THE REAGAN
BLOCK GRANTS

What Have We Learned?

THE REAGAN BLOCK GRANTS
What Have We Learned?

George E. Peterson
Randall R. Bovbjerg
Barbara A. Davis
Walter G. Davis
Eugene C. Durman
Theresa A. Gullo

The Changing Domestic Priorities Series
John L. Palmer and Isabel V. Sawhill, Editors

THE URBAN INSTITUTE PRESS · WASHINGTON, D.C.

Copyright © 1986
THE URBAN INSTITUTE
2100 M Street, N.W.
Washington, D.C. 20037

Library of Congress Cataloging in Publication Data
The Reagan block grants.

(Changing domestic priorities)
1. Block grants—United States.   2. Federal aid to
public welfare—United States.   3. Federal aid to health
planning—United States.   I. Peterson, George E.
II. Bovbjerg, Randall R.   III. Urban Institute.
IV. Series: Changing domestic priorities series.
HJ275.R325   1986   353.0084   86-7791
ISBN 0-87766-400-5 (pbk.)

Printed in the United States of America
9 8 7 6 5 4 3 2 1

THE URBAN INSTITUTE is a nonprofit policy research and educational organization established in Washington, D.C., in 1968. Its staff investigates the social and economic problems confronting the nation and government policies and programs designed to alleviate such problems. The Institute disseminates significant findings of its research through the publications program of its Press. The Institute has two goals for work in each of its research areas: to help shape thinking about societal problems and efforts to solve them, and to improve government decisions and performance by providing better information and analytic tools.

Through work that ranges from broad conceptual studies to administrative and technical assistance, Institute researchers contribute to the stock of knowledge available to public officials and to private individuals and groups concerned with formulating and implementing more efficient and effective government policy.

Conclusions or opinions expressed in Institute publications are those of the authors and do not necessarily reflect the views of other staff members, officers or trustees of the Institute, advisory groups, or any organizations that provide financial support to the Institute.

THE CHANGING DOMESTIC PRIORITIES SERIES

Listed below are the titles available in the Changing Domestic Priorities Series

Books

THE REAGAN EXPERIMENT
  *An Examination of Economic and Social Policies under the Reagan
  Administration* (1982), John L. Palmer and Isabel V. Sawhill, editors

HOUSING ASSISTANCE FOR OLDER AMERICANS
  The Reagan Prescription (1982), James P. Zais, Raymond J. Struyk, and Thomas
  Thibodeau

MEDICAID IN THE REAGAN ERA
  Federal Policy and State Choices (1982), Randall R. Bovbjerg and John Holahan

WAGE INFLATION
  Prospects for Deceleration (1983), Wayne Vroman

OLDER AMERICANS IN THE REAGAN ERA
  Impacts of Federal Policy Changes (1983), James R. Storey

FEDERAL HOUSING POLICY AT PRESIDENT REAGAN'S MIDTERM
  (1983), Raymond J. Struyk, Neil Mayer, and John A. Tuccillo

STATE AND LOCAL FISCAL RELATIONS IN THE EARLY 1980s
  (1983), Steven D. Gold

THE DEFICIT DILEMMA
  Budget Policy in the Reagan Era (1983), Gregory B. Mills and John
  L. Palmer

HOUSING FINANCE
  A Changing System in the Reagan Era (1983), John A. Tuccillo with John L.
  Goodman, Jr.

PUBLIC OPINION DURING THE REAGAN ADMINISTRATION
  National Issues, Private Concerns (1983), John L. Goodman, Jr.

RELIEF OR REFORM?
  Reagan's Regulatory Dilemma (1984), George C. Eads and Michael Fix

THE REAGAN RECORD
  An Assessment of America's Changing Domestic Priorities (1984), John L. Palmer
  and Isabel V. Sawhill, editors (Ballinger Publishing Co.)

ECONOMIC POLICY IN THE REAGAN YEARS
  (1984), Charles F. Stone and Isabel V. Sawhill

URBAN HOUSING IN THE 1980s
  Markets and Policies (1984), Margery Austin Turner and Raymond J. Struyk

MAKING TAX CHOICES
  (1985), Joseph J. Minarik

AMERICA'S CHILDREN: WHO CARES?
Growing Needs and Declining Assistance in the Reagan Era (1985),
Madeleine H. Kimmich

TESTING THE SOCIAL SAFETY NET
The Impact of Changes in Support Programs during the Reagan Administration
(1985), Martha R. Burt and Karen J. Pittman

REAGAN AND THE CITIES
(1986), edited by George E. Peterson and Carol W. Lewis

PERSPECTIVES ON THE REAGAN YEARS
(1986), edited by John L. Palmer

THE REAGAN BLOCK GRANTS
What Have We Learned? (1986)
George E. Peterson, Randall R. Bovbjerg, Barbara A. Davis, Walter G. Davis,
Eugene C. Durman, and Theresa A. Gullo

Conference Volumes

THE SOCIAL CONTRACT REVISITED
Aims and Outcomes of President Reagan's Social Welfare Policy (1984), edited
by D. Lee Bawden

NATURAL RESOURCES AND THE ENVIRONMENT
The Reagan Approach (1984), edited by Paul R. Portney

FEDERAL BUDGET POLICY IN THE 1980s (1984), edited by
Gregory B. Mills and John L. Palmer

THE REAGAN REGULATORY STRATEGY
An Assessment (1984), edited by George C. Eads and Michael Fix

THE LEGACY OF REAGANOMICS
Prospects for Long-term Growth (1984), edited by Charles R. Hulten and Isabel
V. Sawhill

THE REAGAN PRESIDENCY AND THE GOVERNING OF AMERICA
(1984), edited by Lester M. Salamon and Michael S. Lund

Advisory Board of the
Changing Domestic Priorities Project

CONTENTS

TABLES

FOREWORD

This book is part of The Urban Institute's Changing Domestic Priorities project. The project is examining changes that are occurring in the nation's domestic policies under the Reagan administration and is analyzing the effects of those changes on people, places, and institutions.

When Ronald Reagan campaigned for the presidency, he made rejuvenation of federalism one of his top domestic policy priorities. This goal required restructuring of the financial ties between the federal government and state and local governments.

President Reagan has not achieved the fundamental reforms in federalism that he sought. It now appears that his term in office will end without the large-scale return to the states of those domestic responsibilities that he believed had been mistakenly turned over to the federal government.

The federal grants-in-aid structure has proved resilient. Although the post-World War II pattern of strong and persistent growth in federal aid has been ended by the Reagan administration, the principle of shared funding of many domestic programs between the federal and the state or local governments has survived. The federal grant structure continues to give practical definition to federalism.

Perhaps the most important federal grant reform to be accomplished by the Reagan administration has been the strengthening of block grants. Block grants were viewed by the president as a "half-way station" measure on the road to more sweeping federalism reform. They were meant to remove the federal government's categorical restrictions on how states and localities used federal funds. At the same time, they were part of an administration strategy to restore the states to a primary role in the federal system, since it was state governments that exercised most policy discretion under the block grants. From the beginning, these philosophical objectives of block grants were obscured by their more immediate budget purpose. The Reagan block grants were not introduced in a fiscally neutral background, but were explicit tools for reducing total federal assistance to states and localities. The bundle of programs bound together in a "block grant" typically had funding levels cut from previous allocations.

The political purposes behind the block grants made them controversial. But the partisan politics may well turn out to be the most transient characteristics of the Reagan grant reforms. Beyond ideology and beyond budget cutting, the Reagan block grants have begun to establish a working record of effective administrative reform. There is even a modest political consensus in favor of state policy control over these federal grant programs—not as a harbinger of drastic future rearrangements of intergovernmental responsibilities, but as a more effective means of delivering on program objectives and acknowledging the diversity of conditions in the United States.

This book identifies the practical lessons of the Reagan block grant experiment. As the authors note, more than five years have passed since the introduction of the Reagan block grants, and the time is appropriate to digest the actual experience with these grant reforms. The study carefully examines the history of state and local program spending for those programs folded into the Reagan block grants for health and human services—both spending from the block grants themselves and spending for the same program purposes from other federal funding sources as well as from state and local governments' own funds. Data were collected in the field from state program and budget officials. Expenditure records were complemented by interviews with state and local program officials to determine how the new service delivery arrangements were working in practice.

If sweeping federalist reform seems unlikely in the near future, it is virtually certain (in part because of continuing federal budget pressures) that before long a new generation of federal grant reforms will be undertaken. Now is the right time to take stock of the country's experience with block grants, the principal grant innovation of the Reagan years.

The financial support for this effort provided by The Ford Foundation and by the John D. and Catherine T. MacArthur Foundation is gratefully acknowledged. The original data collection was funded by a contract with the U.S. Department of Health and Human Services.

John L. Palmer
Isabel V. Sawhill
Editors
Changing Domestic Priorities Series

ABOUT THE AUTHORS

Randall R. Bovbjerg is a senior research associate at the Health Policy Center of The Urban Institute. He specializes in health care organization and financing and has in the past worked as a state insurance regulator and local health planner. He coauthored *Medicaid in the Reagan Years* (1982).

Barbara A. Davis, a research associate at the Public Finance Center of The Urban Institute during the research on this book, specializes in finance and program analysis. She currently heads the policy group in the District of Columbia's Budget Office.

Walter Davis is a research associate in the Public Finance and Housing Center at The Urban Institute. His background is in city and regional planning. While at the Institute, he has completed working papers on health and human services block grants, Medicaid and state budget strategies, and transit employee compensation.

Eugene C. Durman is a senior regulatory impact analyst with the U.S. Environmental Protection Agency. He has written extensively in the areas of regulatory change and social and welfare services. His most recent publication addressing public services is *Issues in Competitive Contracting for Social Services* (1985).

Theresa Gullo is an analyst at the Congressional Budget Office. She manages water resource legislation and coordinates state and local government cost estimates for CBO's Budget Analysis Division. She was a research associate with The Urban Institute's Public Finance Center at the time this book was written. Her work focused on intergovernmental finance and capital budgeting.

George E. Peterson is a senior fellow at The Urban Institute, and has directed the Institute's grants-in-aid studies. His most recent book is *Reagan and the Cities*, published by The Urban Institute, which he edited with Carol Lewis.

CHAPTER 1

THE BLOCK GRANTS IN PERSPECTIVE

When Ronald Reagan announced his plan to cut back federal spending in February 1981, few items attracted as much attention as his proposal to consolidate about 90 of the more than 300 categorical program grants providing federal financial assistance to state and local governments into a few block grants, at significantly reduced funding levels.

Five years have passed since this presidential initiative, and it is now possible to take stock of how block grants have changed the federal aid picture. Like most federal initiatives announced amid great expectations and great apprehensions, the block grants have revealed more subtlety of coloration in practice than was anticipated. Some of those who most feared state replacement of the federal government in social program responsibility have now concluded, partly on the basis of the block-grant experience, that states have shown far more capacity and willingness to sustain formerly federal programs than they foresaw. Others, who in the first blush of block-grant reform thought grant deregulation would make it possible for states to absorb as much as 20 to 25 percent of the funding reductions through administrative savings alone, have concluded that "waste and inefficiency" were not of this magnitude after all. Still other effects of the block grants have come as a surprise to original supporters and foes alike.

This volume takes a close look at the block-grant experience. Succeeding chapters report in detail on the seven health and human service block grants eventually passed by Congress in 1981. This introductory chapter seeks to place the block grants in policy and budget perspective and to extract the lessons for grant design and federalism appropriate to the five-year experience. It also provides a comparative overview of the impact of the two other block grants—the Education Consolidation and Improvement Act, Chapter 2 pro-

1

vision, and the revamped community development block grant—passed in the first surge of budgetary and federalism reform.

The Political History of Block Grants

The concept of block grants long antedates the Reagan administration and is rooted in perceptions of the defects of the categorical grant system. Proposals to consolidate categorical grants into blocks of programs—permitting more recipient flexibility in setting priorities and imposing fewer administrative burdens on federal executive departments—began shortly after World War II, almost as soon as categorical grant assistance became a significant item in the federal budget. The Cooper-Forand bill introduced in the seventy-ninth Congress (1945–46) would have authorized the states to determine whether to continue federal categorical programs for public assistance or combine the several federal programs into generalized federal support for public welfare, with choices about program design left to the states. In 1949 the first Hoover Commission issued a lengthy critique of categorical assistance programs and concuded, "A system of grants should be established based upon broad categories—such as highways, education, public assistance and public health—as contrasted with the present system of extensive fragmentation."[1]

Administrative Rationalization

As Timothy Conlan pointed out, two quite different strands of reasoning have marked the argument for greater use of block grants.[2] One of these strands accepts the appropriateness of federal priorities but argues that grant programs can be *administered* better, by federal agencies and recipients alike, if narrow categorical restrictions are removed. In Conlan's reconstruction of the historical evolution of the block-grant debate, advocates of administrative rationalization dominated the first twenty years of block-grant proposal.

It was the extraordinary proliferation of categorical grants during the Johnson administration, and the frustrations involved in trying to design programs that would reach from Washington directly to individual cities, that finally created a professional coalition of support for the administrative ne-

1. Commission on the Organization of the Executive Branch, *A Report to Congress on Federal-State Relations* (Washington, D.C.: U.S. Government Printing Office, 1949), pp. 31–32.

2. Timothy J. Conlan, "The Politics of Federal Block Grants: From Nixon to Reagan," *Political Science Quarterly*, vol. 99 (Summer 1984), pp. 247–70.

cessity of categorical grant reform. Jeffrey Pressman and Aaron Wildavsky, among others, tracked the connection between federal program design in Washington and implementation in the field, and concluded that federal program requirements were so complex that, far from enlarging effective federal control over broad program objectives, they enmeshed federal administrators in administrative details that often obscured program goals and frustrated local accomplishment.[3] Soon after he left the Johnson administration as budget director, Charles Schulze concluded: "The ability of a central staff in Washington to judge . . . thousands of local plans . . . and to control their performance is severely limited. . . . I believe that greater decentralization in the government's social programs should and will be made."[4]

The judgments of Pressman-Wildavsky and of Schulze are representative of contemporary criticism both in their content and in the background of the critics. The leading critics of categorical assistance were administrators with broad responsibility like Schultze, academics like Pressman-Wildavsky, and Washington institutions like the Advisory Commission on Intergovernmental Relations and the General Accounting Office, which were outside the system of congressional politics and single-program bureaucracies. Block grants appealed primarily to those who looked at the cumulative total of administrative responsibilities necessary to implement federal categorical programs.

Nixon's New Federalism

The second strand of attack on categorical grants, as identified by Conlan, emerged later and was more overtly political. It was embodied in the Richard M. Nixon proposals for special revenue sharing. This line of criticism portrayed categorical grants as the crucial nexus in the "iron triangle" among special interest groups, Congress, and federal program bureaucrats.[5] Categorical grants were regarded as the ideal instruments of Congress—"the porkiest of the pork" in one Nixon official's description—because they delivered specifically identifiable program benefits to specific and narrowly drawn constituencies for which individual congressmen could take credit. Special revenue sharing sought not only to consolidate federal grant programs, but to eliminate the expansion of federal program priorities, federal mandates, and federal monitoring and reporting requirements through the grant system.

---

3. Jeffrey L. Pressman and Aaron B. Wildavsky, *Implementation* (Berkeley, California: University of California Press, 1973).

4. Charles L. Schultze, *The Politics and Economics of Public Spending* (Washington, D.C.: Brookings Institution, 1968), p. 105.

5. See, for example, David Mayhew, *Congress: The Electoral Connection* (New Haven, Connecticut: Yale University Press, 1974).

In effect, the special revenue sharing proposals sought to loosen the programmatic control of Congress over domestic policy by transferring much of the discretion over program design to the states and localities. As President Nixon stated in the 1971 State-of-the-Union message: "The time has come to reverse the flow of power and resources from the states and communities to Washington, and start power and resources flowing back from Washington to the states and communities and, more important, to the people, all across America."[6]

In the end, the special revenue sharing concept failed because of intensely partisan resistance from Congress. The political science of the administration's grants analysis may have been vindicated, but the congressional commitment to categorical grants proved impossible to dislodge, especially during a period of Democratic control of the House of Representatives.

Perhaps ironically, two of the less sweeping, more administratively oriented block-grant proposals made by Richard Nixon did become law. The community development block grant, which consolidated many of the specifically urban programs of the federal government, had strong support among mayors, who wanted control over the many new programs and new community organizations that the Great Society initiatives had spawned. By 1972, when community development block-grant legislation was passed, virtually all professional analysis recommended some significant consolidation of the Johnson urban programs. The other successful block-grant initiative was the Comprehensive Employment and Training Act (CETA). It consolidated seventeen categorical training programs but retained several "national emphasis" programs within its structure, thereby satisfying the congressional desire for providing program direction. CETA, in particular, began to be recategorized by Congress almost as soon as the block-grant legislation had been passed. So many new categorical programs were added to the "block" grant that by 1977 the block-grant proportion of CETA appropriations had declined to 23 percent.[7]

Expenditure Control

One other strand of political economy marks the history of block grants. Most of the block-grant proposals were made in the context of increased funding. In part, this reflected the general growth in grants-in-aid support.

6. Richard M. Nixon, Second State of the Union Address, delivered on January 22, 1971, in *Congress and the Nation*, vol. 3 (Washington, D.C.: Congressional Quarterly Services, 1972), p. 113b.

7. William Mirengoff and Lester Rindler, *CETA: Manpower Programs under Local Control* (Washington, D.C.: National Academy of Sciences, 1978).

In part, it reflected the political assessment that programmatic opposition to block grants would be easiest to overcome if total funding were increased, thereby reducing the need for individual programs to compete with one another over the allocation of block-grant funds.

However, the hope that program consolidation would slow the *future* growth of federal grants-in-aid funding always was part of the block-grant rationale. The original proposals to consolidate public welfare programs were based, in part, on the conviction that fragmented welfare programs were not only inefficient but far more difficult to control budgetarily. The only block grant passed between the Nixon and Reagan administrations—Title XX for social service programs—involved very little program consolidation. Instead, its principal feature was the ceiling it placed on federal social service expenditures. The Title XX budget ceiling replaced a system of open-ended federal matching of state expenditures for social services that previously had existed.[8] In exchange, the states obtained more freedom in selecting program priorities.

The Reagan Block Grants

The Reagan block-grant proposals emerged from both the administrative and political criticisms of categorical grants and the desire to curb federal spending. In his speech to the joint session of Congress in which he introduced his Program for Economic Recovery, the president promised that block grants would "bring government closer to the people, provide relief from categorical grant programs [that] burden local and state governments with a mass of federal regulations and federal paperwork," and "consolidate programs which are scattered throughout the federal bureaucracy." Indeed, apart from the federal budget cuts that the president imposed, block grants became the most specific embodiment of his new approach to domestic policy.

Congressional Approval

Block-grant approval moved swiftly. The Program for Economic Recovery was announced February 18, 1981. By mid-April the administration presented to Congress in two documents supplementing the original fiscal 1982 budget, a total of six new block grants as well as several changes in existing blocks.[9] By the end of April all the block grants were introduced as legislation in both the House and Senate. Before the end of May, the House

---

8. Martha Derthick, *Uncontrollable Spending for Social Services Grants* (Washington, D.C.: Brookings Institution, 1975).
9. Unless otherwise indicated, fiscal years throughout this volume are federal fiscal years.

approved the administration's block grants without extensive discussion and
without making any significant changes. The Senate, on the other hand, made
numerous and important changes that included a reduction in the number of
blocks and the reestablishment of many of the strings that the administration
had removed and the House had not reintroduced.

The administration had been working from the start to apply the budget
reconciliation process, established in 1974 but little used by previous administrations, to achieve a number of budget changes quickly before Reagan's
postelection popularity faded. Despite the changes that the Senate made to
the block-grant consolidations, the blocks continued as part of the reconciliation process, which the Congress completed on July 29, 1981. The president
signed the Omnibus Budget Reconciliation Act of 1981 on August 13. The
speed of legislative consideration and the use of the reconciliation process
had effectively taken block-grant consideration out of the hands of congressional committees, the groups that, in the Reagan political analysis, were the
ultimate bulwark of the categorical grant system.

The final block-grant legislation provided for nine new or revised block
grants containing fifty-seven categorical grants with fiscal 1982 budget authority of $9.7 billion (see table 1). By some standards the change in the
federal grant structure was modest. The new block grants accounted for only

TABLE 1

REAGAN BLOCK-GRANT CONSOLIDATION, FISCAL YEARS 1981–83

Action and Date	Number of Block Grants	Number of Categorical Grant Programs	1981, Baseline	1982, Carter Administration	1982, Final
				Funding ($ Billions)	
President's proposal	3	90	14.6	15.6	11.4
Administration program	6	84	n.a.	14.7	10.9
Final approval (all block grants)	9	57	11.1	n.a.	9.7

SOURCES: President's proposal—unpublished data, Office of Management and Budget (David
A. Stockman's "black book," January 26, 1981), and President Reagan's "Program
for Economic Recovery," announcement to Congress, February 18, 1981 (see also
Congressional Quarterly Almanac: 97th Congress, 1st Session . . . 1981, Washington, D.C.: Congressional Quarterly Inc., 1981), pp. 245ff); administration program—taken from U.S. Congress, House, Committee on the Budget, *Additional
Details on Budget Savings*, 97 Cong., 1 sess., April 1981; and final approval—from
U.S. Congress, *Omnibus Budget Reconciliation Act 1981* (PL 97-35), 97 Cong., 1
sess., August 13, 1981.

n.a. Not available.

about 10 percent of federal aid to state and local governments, and the programs consolidated into the block grants represented roughly 15 percent of the state and local programs assisted by federal dollars. Nevertheless, even with the Senate-sponsored changes, the Reagan block-grant consolidations represented the most significant grant consolidation yet enacted by Congress.

Structure of the Reagan Block Grants

Several features set the Reagan block grants apart from earlier block-grant efforts. One distinguishing element is the consistently preeminent role assigned to the states in block-grant administration. Earlier block grants did not make a distinction between state and local governments as recipients of federal aid. They intended to consolidate programs at whatever level of government formerly had administered (or supervised) federal categorical program implementation. For social service programs (Title XX), this was the state; for community development, the city; and for manpower training (CETA), either local community-based organizations or the local government.

The Reagan block grants, in contrast, systematically reassigned program and funding control to the states. This reorientation was consistent with the Reagan view of federalism, in which the states are the fundamental unit of the federal system and local governments (and the federal government) exercise only those powers expressly assigned to them by the states. Although Congress imposed guarantees of pass-through funding to localities on some of the block grants, the general transfer of program discretion and administrative authority to the states survived the block-grant modifications made by Congress.

The Reagan block grants also introduced the novel device of permitting transfers of federal funding among block grants and from certain block grants to other federally supported programs in the same field. Table 2 summarizes the principal structural characteristics of the block grants.

Finally, the block grants were assigned a leading role in the campaign to reduce federal domestic spending. In one sense, the public attention given to the block grants may seem out of proportion to their importance, for even as proposed by the president, the new block grants accounted for only about 11 percent of total federal aid to states and localities. However, the block grants became the selected instrument in the administration's attempts to reduce the domestic budget. Table 3 shows the burden of funding reductions proposed to be borne by the block grants.[10] More important, the president

---

10. Funding for the block grants, as enacted by Congress, and with all fiscal 1982 supplements, fell by approximately 8 percent from 1981 categorical grant levels.

TABLE 2

SUMMARY OF SELECTED BLOCK-GRANT FEATURES

Block Grant	Relation to Previous Categorical Grant Programs	Funding Levels (Budget Authority)	Transition Provisions	Special Provisions	Transferability
Social Services	Replaces XX and XX training and child day care monies	Fiscal 1982: 2.40 billion (19.3 percent less than in fiscal 1981). No match required. Fiscal 1984: 2.70 billion	States must assume on October 1, 1981, or money lapses	Eliminates requirement that half of the federal monies go to welfare recipients	Up to 10 percent can be tranferred to health or energy block grants
Low-income home energy assistance	Replaces low-income energy assistance	Fiscal 1982: 1.87 billion (1.3 percent increase from fiscal 1981). No match required. Fiscal 1984: 2.10 billion	States must assume on October 1, 1981, or money lapses	Up to 15 percent may be used for weatherization. "Reasonable amount for energy crisis" services	Up to 10 percent can be transferred to health, community services or social services block grants
Community services	Replaces Community Services Administration programs, directed toward governments and agencies	Fiscal 1982: 348 million (32.8 percent less than in fiscal 1981). No match required. Fiscal 1984: 348 million	State may assume at the beginning of any quarter beginning October 1, 1981, through October 1, 1982. After October 1982, money lapses if the state does not assume administrative responsibility	For fiscal 1982 and fiscal 1983: 90 percent of resources must go to previous grantees	5 percent may be tranferred to Head Start, energy, or programs for older Americans

Alcohol, drug abuse, and mental health	Consolidates ten categorical programs: drug abuse community services, alcoholism treatment and rehabilitation, alcohol formula grants, drug abuse formula grants, grants to community mental health centers (CHMCs)	Fiscal 1982: 432 million (26.2 percent less than in fiscal 1981). No match required; federal funds must not supplant state and local funds. Fiscal 1984: 469 million	Same as community services	CMHCs funded in 1980 and categorically eligible in block-grant year to be funded. Mental health and substance abuse funds to be split according to pre-block shares Alcohol and drug programs each to get 35 percent of substance abuse "mini block," with remaining 30 percent split at state discretion	7 percent may be transferred to other health block grants
Preventive health and health services	Consolidates one block grant and six categorical programs: Health Incentive Grant, Rape Crisis Centers, Urban Rodent Control, Fluoridation, Health Education and Risk Reduction, Emergency Medical Services, Home Health	Fiscal 1982: 81.6 million (12.4 percent less than in fiscal 1981). No match required; federal funds must not supplant state and local funds. Fiscal 1984: 88.2 million	Same as community services	Hypertension function must be funded in 1982 at 75 percent of 1981 level, lower thereafter Rape prevention funding is earmarked as not reallocable to other functions	7 percent may be transferred to other health block grants

TABLE 2 (Continued)

Block Grant	Relation to Previous Categorical Grant Programs	Funding Levels (Budget Authority)	Transition Provisions	Special Provisions	Transferability
Preventive health and health services (continued)				Emergency Medical Services projects funded in fiscal 1981 must be funded under the block grant in fiscal 1982	
Maternal and child health	Consolidates eight categorical programs: Crippled Children's Services, Disabled Children (SSI), Sudden Infant Death Syndrome, Hemophilia Centers, Lead-Based Paint Prevention, Genetic Diseases, Adolescent Pregnancy, Maternal and Child Health	Fiscal 1982: 373.7 million (17.8 percent less than in fiscal 1982). States must spend $3 of own funds for every $4 received. Fiscal 1984: 399 million	Same as community services	Based on previous allocations, "reasonable proportion" of funds must go to each function Federal set-aside of 15 percent for fiscal 1982 use to fund genetic disease, hemophilia, research training, special projects of regional and national significance "Special consideration to existing projects	No funds may be transferred to other block grant

Elementary and secondary education	Consolidates twenty-three categorical programs, including: Emergency School Aid, School Libraries, Improving Local Educational Practice, Strengthening State Agency Management, Basic Skills Improvement	Fiscal 1982: 437 million (13.7 percent less than in fiscal 1981) Fiscal 1984: 500 million	80 percent passed through local education agencies Government must appoint State Advisory Committee Local education agencies must provide funds to private as well as public schools	No transfers
Community development	Restructures existing community development block grant Shifts control over small cities portion of block grant from federal government to states	Fiscal 1982: 3,400 million Small cities—1,020 million (+ 10 percent from fiscal 1981) Entitlement cities—2,380 million (−10.7 percent from fiscal 1981) Fiscal 1984: 3,468 million	Administration proposed relaxing regulatory requirement that funds be targeted on a low- and moderate-income population; Congress eventually reimposed targeting Local governments apply to states on project basis	No transfers

SOURCES: Funding from Office of Management and Budget Special Analysis H, *Budget of the United States Government,* fiscal years 1983 and 1986 (Washington, D.C.: Government Printing Office); and Office of Management and Budget, unpublished disaggregation of Special Analysis H tables. Other information from *Omnibus Budget Reconciliation Act 1981.*

TABLE 3

COMPARISON OF REAGAN BUDGET REQUESTS FOR FISCAL 1982 WITH ACTUAL
FISCAL 1981 PROGRAM EXPENDITURES
(Budget Authority, in Billions)

Program Category	1981 Expenditures	1982 Reagan Request	Percentage Change, 1981–82
Total block grants	18.7	14.8	−21
New block-grant proposals/ prior categorical spending	14.6	11.4	−22
Total federal aid to state and local governments	94.8	86.2	−9
Major entitlements[a]	311.4	335.3	8
Total domestic spending[b]	511.2	546.1	7
National defense	182.4	226.3	24
Total federal spending	718.4	772.4	8

SOURCE: Block grants and federal aid are from *Budget of the United States Government, Budget Appendix*, and *Special Analysis*, appropriate years. Other data are from Timothy J. Conlan, "The Politics of Federal Block Grants: From Nixon to Reagan," *Political Science Quarterly*, vol. 99 (Summer 1984), pp. 247–70.
   a.   Including social security.
   b.   Total federal spending minus defense and international affairs.

announced that block grants lay at the heart of his budget strategy. He promised to continue to propose block-grant consolidations that would trade greater state-local program flexibility for reduced federal program spending.

Evaluating the Effects of Block Grants

It is a truism of social science that the time is never quite right for policy evaluation. It is either too early, when the observer runs the risk of confusing temporary adjustments with more permanent ones, or too late, when specific program initiatives have dissolved into the general background of other influences.

Nonetheless, a four-year empirical perspective, such as the one taken here, seems approximately right for examining the effects of block grants. It allows for at least one round of evolution in program implementation, while not becoming too far removed from the origins of change. In this section we draw some general conclusions about block grants based on data collected during the first four program years.

The data for this study are drawn largely from an Urban Institute survey of state spending and program adjustments to the block grants in eighteen states from fiscal 1981 through fiscal 1984. The states were selected to provide variation in geography, population size, and fiscal condition. Information was collected from state agencies also regarding spending and program adjustments made by local governments. Except where these adjustments are directly influenced by state laws or regulations, however, state monitoring of local government actions is likely to be incomplete.

State Replacement of Lost Federal Funds

Most states used their own resources to replace at least part of the federal funds lost through block-grant financing reductions. Table 4 shows replacement data throughout fiscal 1984 for the block grants in health and human services for which detailed, comparable data were collected.[11] These show a variety of replacement behavior, ranging from virtually no state replacement of federal monies in the community services block grant (and reinforcing reductions of state funds in many) to sufficient state replacement to maintain *real* levels of program funding in the face of federal aid cuts in several block grants in several states.

The degree of state replacement stands in contrast to early speculation that the states would be unable or unwilling to replace federal grant funds, especially for human service programs that had a dispersed constituency and were not thought to be politically potent. Early studies of the implementation of the block grants seemed to confirm that state governments were not replacing lost human services dollars. Nathan and his associates cited as a major finding in their review of the first-year impact of Reagan policy change in thirteen states, "low overall replacement of lost federal revenues."[12] This finding is consistent with our own early observations on the block grants, in which state replacement was found to be low, especially in states experiencing severe fiscal difficulties.[13]

One reason that state replacement was not more visible in the first year concerns the timing of block-grant implementation in relation to the fiscal year of most states. For most states, planning for their state fiscal 1982 was complete and the state legislature was out of session by the time the block

---

11. The "replacement" funds are a combination of states' own revenues, other federal monies shifted into the block-grant programs, and local funding required or monitored by the state (see chapter 2 for a more detailed discussion). Most replacement spending came from state budgets.

12. Richard P. Nathan, Fred C. Doolittle, and Associates, *The Consequences of Cuts: Effects of the Reagan Domestic Program on State and Local Governments* (Princeton, New Jersey: Princeton University, Urban and Regional Research Center, 1983), p. 191.

13. George E. Peterson, "The State and Local Sector," in John L. Palmer and Isabel V. Sawhill, eds., *The Reagan Experiment: An Examination of Economic and Social Policies under the Reagan Administration* (Washington, D.C.: The Urban Institute, 1982), pp. 157–217.

TABLE 4

STATE REPLACEMENT OF FEDERAL FUNDING CUTS IN HEALTH AND HUMAN SERVICES BLOCK GRANTS,
STATE FISCAL YEARS 1981–84[a]

Measure	Social Services	Community Services	Low-Income Home Energy Assistance	Maternal and Child Health	Preventive Health and Health Services	Alcohol, Drug Abuse, and Mental Health
Number of states for which comparable data are available	18	18	18	11	15	14
Number of states with cuts in federal funds from block grant relative to predecessor categorical grant[b]	17	18	4	3	6	12
Number of states with state government spending increases from state resources	16	1	...	8	9	12
Number of states with total program spending increases[b,c]						
Current dollars	11	1	...	8	8	10
Real dollars[d]	7	0	...	6	4	7

SOURCE: State data as reported to The Urban Institute and the U.S. General Accounting Office.

a. State fiscal years 1981–83 in cases where these are the latest data available.
b. Excludes spending from the Emergency Jobs Appropriations bill. Includes carryover funds.
c. Total program spending includes local spending required by state or monitored by the state, federal block-grant funding, state spending from own resources, and federal categorical funding (Title XIX and Title IVA) used for program purposes.
d. Nominal spending deflated by consumer price index.

grants were finalized by Congress. State legislatures were forced to deal with block grants earlier in anticipation of what they might be like, as both the number of blocks and the programs contained in them were in flux. When the block grants went into effect in October 1981, most states were only months away from beginning the budgeting process for their state fiscal 1983 (starting July 1, 1982). Thus many states made only minimal adjustments until the legislature and the administering agencies could more fully review the state's long-run posture toward the blocks.

Once the states had time to assess the federal program and funding changes, they began to provide greater funding of their own in many program areas. This replacement behavior eventually was made easier by temporary federal assistance through the Emergency Jobs Appropriations bill in 1983 and by the recovery of most state economies beginning in 1984, which lessened state fiscal pressures. As is shown in subsequent chapters, several states also called upon local governments to finance more of the total cost of human service delivery that was eligible for block-grant funding.

State funding replacement was not restricted to the block grants. Although replacement outside of the block-grant programs was not as strong, states also made efforts to replace part of the federal cutbacks in welfare eligibility and in other categorical supports for the poor, especially Medicaid.[14] The block grants can be interpreted in part as a test of states' political commitment in deciding whether or not to sustain human service programs, even when not obliged to do so by the federal government and when no longer subsidized to do so by categorical matching grants. The states passed this test of commitment to a greater degree than most observers anticipated.

Matching Grant Incentives

The funding response of states also sheds light on the effect that more general removal of matching-grant provisions is likely to have on program spending levels. One of the principal features of block grants is the elimination of price incentives to recipient spending. Under a block grant, the amount of federal assistance is fixed as an entitlement and not altered by local or state spending behavior. By contrast, categorical matching grants create a price incentive for greater recipient spending as long as the matching terms are in effect. A matching requirement of 25 percent state to the 75 percent federal funds, as prevailed in Title XX before its conversion to the social services

---

14. Richard P. Nathan and Fred C. Doolittle, *Effects of the Reagan Domestic Program on States and Localities* (Princeton, New Jersey: Princeton University, Urban and Regional Research Center, June 1984).

block grant, for example, made it possible for a state government to generate $1 of additional total spending through the commitment of only 25¢ from its own budget.

The conversion from categorical matching grants to block grants, therefore, might be expected not only to fail to stimulate state replacement of federal funding but to provide a strong incentive to *reduce* spending from states' own resources, by removing the price incentives that helped stimulate state expenditures in the first place.[15]

In reality, almost all programs supported by federal matching grants (except Medicaid and Aid to Families with Dependent Children, AFDC) have now been capped—that is, maximum levels of outlays have been set for which federal matching is available. This capping restricts the stimulative effect of the matching grant structure. For states whose spending exceeds the federal matching limit, price incentives do not exist at the margin under the matching grant structure to further increase program expenditures. Nor does the conversion from matching grants to block grants remove an effective incentive to state spending. In contrast, states whose spending had not reached the matching limit, or which are just at the maximum matching amount, *do* receive effective price subsidies from matching grants. For them, conversion to the block-grant structure can be expected to have a more visible, depressing effect on program spending levels.

A comparison of states' spending adjustments during the conversion from Title XX to the social services grant illustrates these effects. The five states in our sample that were spending in fiscal 1981 at approximately the minimum level required for full federal Title XX matching *cut* their average social services expenditures from own resources by 5.3 percent. The remaining thirteen states *raised* their average social services expenditures from own resources by 18.8 percent.

State Program Priorities

Did states embrace the opportunity to assert new program priorities, and assume new program responsibilities, once freed from federal restrictions and detailed program guidelines? To a significant degree, yes. In fact, the vigorous substitution of state for federal priorities was sometimes a matter of controversy in localities with programs that formerly had been directed by the federal government.

---

15. Wallace E. Oates, "Response: the Economics of the New Federalism," in William Craig Stubblebine and Thomas D. Willett, *Reaganomics: A Midterm Report* (San Francisco: Institute for Contemporary Studies, 1983).

As a rule, the programs that fared best under block-grant consolidation were those with statewide application and a history of state as well as federal funding. The former grantees under such programs were likely to be known to political officials and state agency administrators. A state's willingness to fund these programs in the past, even as part of a required match, established some funding presumption for the future. Similarly, having had substantial control over the program design of a certain activity, a state was likely to assign it a higher priority in budget competition than an activity that the state simply carried out under federal mandate or an activity that had been carried out through federal funding by a third party (for example, by contract).

This principle may be seen at work in the sorting out of program priorities within individual block grants. Within the maternal and child health block grant, the Crippled Children's Services program was one with a long history of state involvement and one that was mentioned for public support in hearings throughout most states. Its share of funding grew. At the other extreme, the Lead-Based Paint program was widely viewed as a big-city program that had been formerly administered by the federal government without state involvement. In almost all states funding for it declined after the introduction of the block grant. Under the preventive health and health services block grant, the Rodent Control program declined for the same reason; it was viewed as a narrowly focused, big-city program with little history of state involvement. (Every rule has its conspicuous exception. In Florida, the Rodent Control program became a political demand of the Hispanic population, and the state responded by augmenting the program with federal funds.) On the scale of entire block grants, the community services block grant received least state support, largely because its federal predecessor program had channeled funds directly to local Community Action Agencies, mostly in cities, with little state program involvement.

States expressed new program priorities for other reasons. When the small-cities portion of the community development block grant shifted from federal to state control, the states gave much greater emphasis to economic development and infrastructure projects than the federal government had done, and much less emphasis to housing rehabilitation.[16] In part, this shift in priorities reflected states' economic difficulties in 1982 and 1983 and the emphasis they gave to economic development throughout their budgets. In part, it also reflected the housing orientation of the federal Department of

---

16. U.S. Department of Housing and Urban Development, *Consolidated Annual Report to Congress on Community Development Programs* (Washington, D.C.: HUD, Office of Assistant Secretary for Planning and Development, 1983), p. 59 and the counterpart volume for 1984.

Housing and Urban Development, which had stamped its own priorities on the predecessor program.

The Education Consolidation and Improvement Act, Chapter Two provision, saw perhaps the greatest change in program emphasis. The single largest program folded into the Chapter 2 provision was federal support for local school desegregation. This was a highly targeted program that concentrated payments on central-city school districts. Under the block grant few states tried to maintain the same degree of targeting, and local school districts did not consider it appropriate to preserve the same programmatic emphasis. Consolidated block-grant funds have been devoted to more general educational purposes; the single largest use has involved purchases of computer equipment.[17] School desegregation lost funding for a number of reasons, one being that it was politically unpopular—even in the cities in which the money was available.

Targeting: Did the Poor and Needy Lose a Disproportionate Share of Funding?

No part of the original debate over the block grants generated more controversy than differing speculations about what would happen to program targeting to the poor, minorities, and those defined as needy under specific federal aid programs. This dilemma was symbolized in starkly conflicting testimony offered to the House Education and Labor Committee in March 1981 by Health and Human Services Secretary Richard S. Schweiker and by Representative Shirley Chisholm. Schweiker maintained that freeing states from federal guidelines would permit them to focus their efforts more effectively on the truly needy, including the poorest members of society. He expected states to respond to funding reductions, too, by targeting program benefits more tightly.[18]

Chisholm, in contrast, expressed acute concern for the fate of programs intended to help poor people if those programs were turned over to the states. She said:

---

17. Regina M. J. Kyle, "Kaleidoscopes II: The Implementation and Impact of the Education Consolidation and Improvement Act in Nine Selected States," (n.p.: E.H. White and Company, Report to the National Institute of Education, May 1985); U.S. Congress, House, Hearing before Subcommittee of the Committee on Government Operations, "Federal Education Assistance: Are Block Grants Meeting the Need?" 98th Cong., 1st sess., September 1983.

18. Richard Schweiker, Secretary of the Department of Health and Human Services, Testimony before U.S. Congress, House, Committee on Education and Labor, 97th Cong., 1st sess., March 31, 1981.

The caucus believes that any budget proposal which gives states total discretion to "establish their own priorities" for social service programs would be a disaster for the poor.

We come to that conclusion on the basis of historical patterns in this country. . . .

We would urge the committee to remember that the poor would clearly be endangered by a block Grant system of social service funding. The probability that funds will be shifted from survival programs into programs that appeal to the middle-class voters or local power structures is all too great.[19]

The actual record of state behavior under the block grants defies easy categorization as to whether targeting to the poor has increased or declined. There have been at least three relevant responses.

First, where income eligibility for programs has been continued but the eligibility levels have been adjusted, the changes almost without exception have been to tighten eligibility standards—that is, to focus the reduced level of total program benefits more narrowly on the poor. For example, several states lowered the income eligibility level for participating in state-financed day care programs, while other states introduced sliding fee schedules for day care that had the effect of targeting dollar benefits more narrowly on the poorest families. These state responses helped protect the very poor but forced those at the margin of income eligibility to make greater adjustments.

Second, the mix of programs provided under the block grants seems to have shifted from programs directed toward people eligible on an income basis to those eligible on other grounds. A case study in chapter 2 of this volume shows how emphatically Virginia shifted its social services priorities from programs provided on an income-eligible basis to programs provided without regard to income. This shift was not the one Representative Chisholm feared, in which middle-income families indulged themselves with discretionary social services, but rather a shift to a new definition of "most needy" that gave priority to protective services for children and adults where income was not an element of need. This shift was made easier by elimination after the initiation of block grants of the former federal requirement that at least one-half of all federal funds be used to support categorically eligible individuals—those eligible because of their participation in AFDC or other federal categorical programs.

In the community development block grant, the shift from housing rehabilitation programs to economic development programs and infrastructure, at states' initiative, appears to have resulted in lower proportions of benefits being directly targeted upon low- and moderate-income families—though this

---

19. Representative Shirley Chisholm, Testimony before U.S. Congress, House, Committee on Education and Labor, 97th Cong., 1st sess., March 31, 1981.

proportion of the beneficiary class remains very high.[20] The shift was made easier by administration actions to remove or soften the income-targeting requirements of the community development block grant. If the administration's initial proposal to eliminate income targeting altogether as a mandatory criterion for allocating funds from this block grant within cities had survived challenge, a much more vigorous reallocation of direct benefits would have been expected.[21]

In education, states retreated from the previous federal targeting that focused funds especially on big-city schools with large minority populations. The new education block grant distributes federal funds to the states on the basis of school population, and most states distribute funds to local school districts on the same basis. Only seventeen states target their education block grant aid to local education agencies based on the concentration of children with greatest needs.[22] In effect, most states have endorsed the view that, when it comes to education, all children are needy.

The discussion thus far has been of program-specific allocations within the block grants. At a larger scale of comparison, a third effect of the block grants was to shift the general mix of the federal aid structure away from populations with special needs. (Henderson, in her study of the education block grant, presents a revealing picture of the distribution of federal assistance for education (see table 5.)[23] The data show that the Reagan years have put a halt to a fifteen-year trend in which federal aid for programs for special populations grew much faster than aid for programs for general populations. Starting from rough parity in 1965, federal funding for special populations was approximately three times higher than federal aid for general populations by 1980. In contrast, since 1981 the growth in federal funding for special needs populations has been somewhat *less* than that for general school populations. The Chapter 2 block-grant replacement of emergency (desegregation) school aid was an important part of arresting the past trend by deemphasizing targeting to special populations.

Reaching an overall conclusion regarding the impacts of the block grants on targeting to the poor is admittedly speculative because not all provisions of all block grants worked in a single direction. A reading of the evidence

---

20. U.S. General Accounting Office, *States Are Making Good Progress in Implementing the Small Cities CDBG Program* (Washington, D.C.: U.S. Government Printing Office, September 1983).

21. Neil S. Mayer, "Community Development Block Grants: Missing the Target, working paper (Washington, D.C.: Urban Institute, June 1984).

22. Anne Henderson, *Anything Goes: A Summary Report on Chapter 2*, NCEE Occasional Paper, (Washington, D.C.: National Committee for Citizens in Education, 1985), pp. 42–44.

23. Ibid.

TABLE 5

FEDERAL SPENDING BY TYPE OF ELEMENTARY AND SECONDARY EDUCATION
PROGRAM, FISCAL YEARS 1966–84
(Thousands)

Program	1966	1972	1977	1981	1984 (Estimate)
Programs for special populations					
Compensatory Education for the Disadvantaged	746,904	1,570,388	1,929,775	3,235,977	3,487,500
Bilingual Education	. . .	26,010	96,549	168,000	169,183
Handicapped	4,918	67,933	210,595	914,718	1,239,415
Desegregation Aid	5,291	92,214	229,300	385,509	. . .
Follow Through	. . .	2,024	57,600	59,800	14,767
Indian Education	. . .	. . .	48,090	83,038	68,780
Total	757,113	1,758,569	2,571,909	4,847,042	4,979,645
Programs for general populations					
Block grant and other nontargeted aid	168,270	272,683	372,937	382,565	450,655
Impact Aid	409,593	648,608	764,628	553,942	565,000
Vocational Aid	128,468	416,945	534,305	682,213	738,475
Total	706,331	1,338,236	1,671,870	1,618,720	1,754,130

SOURCE: Anne Henderson, *Anything Goes: A Summary Report on Chapter 2*, NCCE Occasional
Paper (Washington, D.C.: National Committee for Citizens in Education, 1985),
p. 64.

indicates that, in general, programs with income eligibility requirements have
seen their eligibility standards tightened, but that other criteria have supplanted
family income levels in allocating significant amounts of federal and state
funding under the block grants.

Targeting to Big Cities

Cities have been one of the clearest losers of federal funds under block
grants. Probably the most sizable losses were felt by big-city public school
districts with the elimination of desegregation funding upon consolidation of
education programs into the education block grant. However, the big-city
entitlement share of the community development block grant was also cut.
Several of the human service and health programs targeted to cities suffered
especially steep reductions compared to other programs that were consolidated
into the block grants, although the Emergency Jobs Appropriations bill of

1983 restored funding and in some states targeted funding in high-unemployment areas.[24]

To some degree the diversion of aid from cities may reflect residual resentment on the part of states toward big cities, or, in the case of the education block grant, a lessened federal priority for a specific big-city problem. To a greater degree, the adjustments seem to reflect a conviction that cities generally had gained a more favorable place in the federal grant structure than their objective situation merited.

Between fiscal years 1981 and 1984 the average share of community service block grant allocations received by the largest Community Action Agency of each state in the sample (almost always a big-city agency) fell from 27 percent to 19 percent of the state total. But on closer inspection, the shifts in funding can be seen to come *closer* to the geographical distribution of poverty, not to move farther away from it. For example, in 1981 Detroit received roughly 50 percent of Michigan's total Community Action Program payments, while the city represented only 25 percent of the state's poor. In 1983 the Detroit Community Action Agency received just under 43 percent of total community services block grant funding, and state policy is to bring Detroit's allocation to the 25 percent "poverty share" over a period of years. Other states show this pattern as well. In California, the Los Angeles share of the community services block grant was reduced from 36 percent to 27 percent of the total, while Chicago's share was reduced from 67 percent to 41 percent. In both cases, the states moved to conform their allocations more closely to local poverty shares—as they interpreted the purpose of the community services block grant program.

The community development block grant offers another example of reallocation away from cities that, at the same time, is consistent with other needs criteria. When the small cities' portion of the community development block grant was transferred from federal to state control, one of the first consequences was to spread funding among a larger number of local governments. (Under both federal and state administration of the small-cities program, grants to local recipients are made in response to local project applications.) However, close examination of the pattern of local funding allocations in thirteen states showed that state awards actually were *more effectively targeted on distressed communities*, using the federal Department of Housing and Urban Development's own criteria for measuring community distress, than

---

24. This bill was a congressional response to the recession; it appropriated $4.9 billion to create jobs and provide assistance to the unemployed.

were the federal government's awards.[25] One reason for this outcome was that many more communities were drawn into grant application for the first time under state administration of the small-city community development block grant.

Administrative and Program Savings

In the initial enthusiasm for block-grant advocacy, several administration spokesmen claimed that the funding cuts would be offset virtually in their entirety by the administrative savings that block grant simplification would make possible.

In testimony delivered on April 28, 1981, before the Manpower and Housing Subcommittee, David Stockman said:

> The compound impact of duplicative effort, applicant costs, and client dissatisfaction is what this Administration believes the block grant approach will allow States to successfully address. . . . Aggregate funding for the programs being consolidated will be reduced from current service levels under the block grants. However, the services delivered need not be diminished because massive reductions in Federal administrative requirements also are being made.[26]

When Health and Human Services Secretary Schweiker was asked for his estimates of the administrative savings to be expected at the state level by adopting the block-grant approach, he responded by saying:

> Well, I think that is a very important point . . ., because some of the leading State health officials have really felt that they are so hamstrung and so handicapped—and these are states with active health departments—that they can really save a significant amount of money.
>
> For example, Governor Bond's—whose State (Missouri) has a very fine program—health director for the State is quoted as saying that one in five of his employees today works to comply with the Federal regulations of the more than 40 health programs funded by Washington, and that he predicted that he could do a better job with 75 percent of the funds he now gets from Washington if he did not have the Federal mandates that go with them. . . .
>
> The point is that there is significant savings for those States involved; and a lot of them say it will be 25 percent. I do not represent that it will be, but I think there is certainly significant savings in some of the States in these areas.[27]

After three years of implementation experience, most states have concluded that the block grants, as promised, have substantially reduced paper-

---

25. Charlotte Bienson, "State vs. Federal Allocation of Small-City CDBG Awards (New York: State University of New York at Buffalo, 1984).

26. David Stockman, Testimony before U.S. Congress, House, Subcommittee on Manpower and Housing, 97th Cong., 1st sess., April 28, 1981.

27. Schweiker, testimony before the House Education and Labor Committee.

work. The General Accounting Office reported that officials in almost two-thirds of its sample of thirteen states believed that the time and effort spent in preparing program applications had been reduced, and almost three-fourths spent less time and effort in reporting to the federal government.[28] Few states had any documentation, or even would make claims, regarding the magnitude of dollar savings resulting from less paperwork, though all characterized it as small relative to initial federal funding reductions.

The largest paperwork savings were claimed in eligibility determination. Many states abandoned case-by-case determination of program eligibility, and its attendant paperwork, in favor of self-designation within broad geographic neighborhoods or other broad groupings. The Title XX eligibility process had been particularly complex, since federal funds had to be devoted to categorically eligible families. This rule required a family-by-family determination of eligibility by ascertaining whether the family received assistance under federal welfare programs. Several states, when freed from this requirement, decided to provide certain social services to any family in a designated area that requested those services. Florida claimed $4.8 million in annual savings (equal to about 30 percent of its initial funding reduction for Title XX) by switching from family-to-family eligibility investigation to eligibility for all families in designated areas.

States also found opportunities to consolidate the administration of federal grant programs within the states' own program administration, once the separate constraints on federal programs were removed. The alcohol, drug abuse, and mental health block grant offered possibilities for such administrative rationalization. Almost every state already offered its own alcoholism treatment and prevention programs, its own programs aimed at curbing drug abuse, and its own system of mental health centers. Federal funding for parallel activities always had been a small part of the total, but one that had to be administered separately because of federal program mandates and reporting requirements. Every state in the sample stated that it had achieved some administrative consolidation under the alcohol, drug abuse, and mental health block grant, usually by collapsing the federal program within the existing state administrative apparatus.

Program Standards

The attention paid to savings in paperwork may have diverted attention from a more important cost issue raised by the block grants—namely, the

---

28. U.S. General Accounting Office, *Block Grants: Overview of Experiences to Date and Emerging Issues* (Washington, D.C.: U.S. Government Printing Office, April 1985).

ability of states to reduce program costs by reducing service standards. Part of the Reagan block-grant philosophy was to substitute state regulation of service standards for federal regulation. Illustrative of the potential difference in standards are regulations pertaining to infant and toddler day care. Since 1968 the federal government had followed an erratic course in proposing, modifying, and reconsidering day care regulations.[29] As of 1980, minimum standards had been preliminarily approved in the form of federal interagency day care requirements, and these had been incorporated in many state programs in anticipation of a decision to make them federal mandates. However, the day care requirements were expressly withdrawn as part of the social services block-grant consolidation.

The program impact of this step may be gauged by comparing the proposed federal day care requirements with those selected by Texas in 1982. Texas, for a time, had adhered to proposed requirements in its Title XX day care. When the federal requirements were finally eliminated, Texas managed to care for about 16 percent more children in day care at almost 20 percent less total cost to the state. But in the process Texas altered drastically the minimum ratios of staff to children, as can be seen from table 6. Although Texas is an extreme case, only three states in 1982 had staffing ratio requirements for infant day care as high as the 1980 proposed federal requirements for toddler care. Only one state, Massachusetts, met the staff-child ratio for both infants and toddlers.[30]

The present study did not attempt to make independent judgments about the service quality being offered by the states in day care or any other field. However, the policy debate over day care regulations suggests that truly large savings in costs of services must be acquired at the expense of other service characteristics. Cost savings do not accrue from the elimination of paperwork alone.

Cash Carryovers

One lesson in grant administration learned from the block-grant experience concerns the magnitude of cash carried over from one fiscal year to the next. During the first investigations of the effects of block grants, observers

29. James Nelson, "The Politics of Federal Day Care Regulations," in E. Zigler and E. Gordon, eds., *Day Care: Scientific and Social Policy Issues* (Boston, Massachusetts: Auburn House, 1982).

30. Kathryn T. Young and Edward Zigler, "Infant and Toddler Day Care: Regulation and Policy Implications" unpublished paper (New Haven, Connecticut: Yale University, 1985).

TABLE 6

PROPOSED FEDERAL DAY CARE STANDARDS AND TEXAS STANDARDS, 1982

Requirement	Federal Interagency Day Care Standard	Texas Standard
Minimum staff-to-child ratio		
Infant	1:3	1:5 to 1:7
Toddler	1:4	1:9 to 1:13
Minimum group size	6	Not specified
Infant	6	Not specified
Toddler	12	35
Staff training		
Director	Specialized training in child care	No
Caregiver	Specialized training in child care	No

SOURCE: Kathryn T. Young and Edward Zigler, "Infant and Toddler Day Care: Regulation and Policy Implications," unpublished document (New Haven, Connecticut: Yale University, 1985).

noted that many states had been able to avoid making extreme spending adjustments by committing funds that remained unexpended from the old categorical grants, in addition to their new block-grant receipts. At the same time, this was interpreted as a transitional phenomenon. The federal government had made advance payments on some categorical programs, which it did not seek to recapture, and during the period when block grants were first introduced some overlap occurred between the old categorical funding cycles and the new fiscal-year block-grant entitlements.

After three years of block-grant implementation, however, cash carryovers remain high. It is now apparent that the states have responded to federal funding uncertainty by husbanding cash wherever possible. This strategy allows the states to smooth out program spending adjustments, even in the face of what they fear may be sudden elimination of federal grant support. The low-income housing energy assistance block grant has been the favorite vehicle for banking carryover cash because it permits the most liberal transfer of funds to other block grants. Consequently, the states have used it as a means of storing funds until program funding priorities become clearer. Several health block grants also expressly permit carryovers and have been used to bank federal grant payments for the future (see table 2, the "Transferability" column for the alcohol, drug abuse, and mental health block grant and the preventive health and health services block grant.)

In assessing future block-grant proposals that consolidate multiyear categorical programs, analysts can anticipate that carryover funds will give the states more financial flexibility than the year-to-year cuts in new federal funding alone would imply. The Reagan administration's policy of allowing states to reallocate carryover categorical funds, within the parameters of the new block grants, enhanced states' flexibility.

Block Grants as Countercyclical Tools

Part of the funds provided by the Emergency Jobs Appropriations bill was directed as supplemental funding for the various block grants. Succeeding chapters of this volume track the use of these funds in individual block grants. The general conclusion that emerges is that the supplemental funds were used in ways very similar to the basic block-grant allocations. Few states modified their routine procedures to try to stimulate job creation, to speed up disbursement of funds to counter high unemployment, or to target intrastate distribution to areas of high unemployment.

Except as a symbolic expression of concern, supplemental funding for the block grants did not prove to be an effective job creation instrument or a countercyclical policy tool.

The Future of Block Grants

In August 1981 congressional approval to the first nine Reagan block grants appeared to be just the beginning of a new era of block-grant consolidation. The president himself announced the administration's intention to continue to propose new block grants and to recommend even broader consolidation into "super" block grants that would give the states very wide authority over program selection.

Since that time the administration has, in fact, made twenty-three proposals to form new block grants or expanded existing ones. Only one such initiative has succeeded—the replacement of CETA by the Job Training Partnership Act in 1982. Why did the momentum toward establishing block grants come to such a sudden halt, and what does the recent history of failed attempts portend for the future?

Grant Reform versus Domestic Budget Cutting

Subsequent proposals for block grants have failed in large part because they have become identified politically as instruments of domestic budget cutting. If the Omnibus Budget Reconciliation Act allowed the first wave of grant consolidations to move through Congress with unprecedented speed, it also indelibly stamped the Reagan block grants with the budget-cutting priority of this budget reconciliation act. The perception that block grants are first and foremost considered by the administration as a device for reducing federal domestic spending has been reinforced by subsequent presidential proposals to reduce funding for the newly created block grants or, in the case of the community services block grant, to terminate the block grant altogether shortly after its creation. Richard Williamson, the White House official who, together with state and local officials, was responsible for negotiating the New Federalism proposals to turn back responsibility to the states, concluded that in the end the perception that budget cutting had top priority made principled consideration of President Reagan's federalism proposals impossible.[31] The administration's procedures used in 1981 to bypass congressional committee consideration of the block grants also engendered a response in Congress that has made the committees even more tenacious in asserting their prerogatives with respect to subsequent block-grant proposals.

There is an element of irony in the fact that block grants now have been subordinated to the politics of the budget debate. The evidence on implementation of the Reagan block grants has successfully answered many of the concerns about states' capacity or commitment to administer grant programs without federal categorical restrictions. Many observers thought that states would simply withdraw from broad areas of domestic policy once free to do so under federal grant regulations. Instead, they have moved to replace the federal presence, albeit selectively and according to their own priorities. It was feared in some quarters that states would give emphasis to redistribution of program benefits from the poor to the middle class. They have not done so. Efficient administration of the block-grant programs was said by some to be beyond states' capacities. The evidence since 1981 is that states have done at least as good a job in administration as the federal government had done formerly. Even the interest groups and service providers with the largest direct stake in the old categorical grant system have reported that they are roughly neutral toward the Reagan block grants as an administrative form after three years of implementation experience.

---

31. Richard S. Williamson, "The 1982 New Federalism Negotiations," *Publius*, vol. 13 (Spring 1983), pp. 11–32.

In a word, the administrative rationale of block-grant consolidation, and even the political rationale for returning decision-making authority to the states, has been largely vindicated by the experience since 1981. But application of these lessons to a new generation of block grants has been paralyzed by the perception that block grants have become, above all, an instrument for reducing domestic program budgets. The same consolidations that might command majority support in the context of budget neutrality have aroused fierce opposition in parts of Congress when proposed as part of domestic budget cuts.

Still, if the budget debate should subside, it is likely that further block-grant initiatives eventually will be authorized. For example, the proposals to consolidate the many forms of mass transit and other transportation aid into a block grant that permits local authorities to exercise their own choices between new capital construction, repair of existing capital facilities, and subsidies for different types of transportation operations would appear to meet the goals of both greater administrative simplicity and greater local control over setting priorities. However, the block-grant proposal has yet to be considered on its intrinsic merits because it has been tied to steep reductions for mass transit funding.

Are Block Grants a Permanent Feature of the Grant System?

A more fundamental challenge to the role of block grants in the federal aid system may be their inherent instability. Categorical grants typically carry a strong expression of federal purpose. When different categorical grants are consolidated into a block grant, these federal objectives remain clearly in mind. The block-grant structure gives the states new flexibility to assign their own emphasis to different federal program goals and to design new ways to achieve these goals. Once a block grant becomes nothing more than a small fraction of a state's general program budget, however, it may seem to lose its rationale for existence. For example, an unrestricted Chapter 2 education block grant that adds less than one-half of 1 percent to state and local educational budgets does not have a clear purpose, and neither does a community development block grant that simply is folded into a much larger state budget for economic development or a preventive health and health services block grant that makes a small federal contribution to a much larger state public health budget.

It is this line of reasoning that has led President Reagan to characterize block grants not as ends in themselves but as halfway stations toward the full federalism goal of turning back to the states complete responsibility for the program areas consolidated into the block grants. A formal "swap" of functions—a "turnback" of selected federal responsibilities to the state and local governments in exchange for relinquishing certain tax sources, such as proposed in the New Federalism—now seems highly unlikely.[32] However, gradual federal abandonment of the block grants as they become integrated into state budgets could accomplish a de facto turnback that is consistent with the Reagan philosophy of government.

There are an alternative possibilities. In the past most block grants gradually have been recategorized by submerging them with new program mandates. Another possibility is to rejuvenate the block-grant structure every four or six years by a fresh expression of broad federal priorities. If the federal government were committed to the principle of avoiding narrow restrictions on state program selection, yet also wanted a vehicle for identifying new priorities within domestic policy, it could use the block grants as deliberate seed money to encourage new state policy approaches. The federal education block grant, for example, could be used to encourage local districts to develop local improvement projects of their own design, rather than merely supplement local budgets in unrestricted fashion.

Organization of the Book

The remaining chapters of this volume consider the record of state adjustments to the health and human service block grants. Each chapter examines the adjustments, then weighs the most important policy issues that implementation of the block grant has raised in the states or localities. The chapters draw on original data collection. (A joint agreement regarding block-grant data collection was made with the U.S. General Accounting Office. In some instances state expenditure information was collected from the states according to a mutually agreed upon format by GAO teams.) No attempt was made to collect original data for the education and the community development block grants, and therefore the discussions do not report on them in detail.

In their analyses of expenditure adjustments, the authors have sought to go beyond the block grants themselves to track *total* funding for the program areas consolidated into the block grants. Such funding may be drawn from the block grants but may also come from other federal funding sources,

---

32. For a summary description of the New Federalism swap and turnback proposals see Williamson, "The 1982 New Federalism Negotiations."

the states' own budgets, or local government sources. The use of the *program* as the organizing unit of analysis has the advantage of both identifying net changes in funding support and acting as a reminder that the ultimate purpose behind budgets is to finance the delivery of program services.

CHAPTER 2

SOCIAL SERVICES

Unlike several of the other block grants, the social services block grant did not require that the states assume responsibility for services previously administered by the federal government. Under the previous Title XX programs, the states had, since October 1, 1975, designed program plans that defined the services to be provided, the organizations to have responsibility for service provision, and the persons eligible to receive those services, within limits set by the federal statute and regulations.[1]

Under both the social services block grant and the previous Title XX program, services were focused broadly on meeting the nonmedical needs of primarily low-income populations. Services and target populations were and continue to be diverse, including day care for children of working parents, information and referral services available "without regard to income," protection against child abuse, and homemaker services to incapacitated adults to delay or prevent entry into a nursing home.[2]

Despite the basic continuity, the social services block grant made several significant changes in the previous Title XX program. The social services block grant, in essence, removed several burdensome constraints to state decision-making from a federal program already under state control. It eliminated the matching requirement of 25 percent state funds to 75 percent federal

---

1. For a summary of events leading to the creation of Title XX, see Paul E. Mott, *Meeting Human Needs: The Social and Political History of Title XX* (Washington, D.C.: National Conference on Social Welfare, 1976). An overview of the functioning of the program with emphasis on legislative involvement is contained in Deborah E. S. Bennington, *A Legislator's Guide to Title XX* (Denver, Colorado: National Conference of State Legislatures, 1978).

2. See U.S. Department of Health and Human Services, *Social Services USA*, DHHS publication HDS-81-02020, (Washington, D.C.: U.S. Government Printing Office, 1979), pp. I-1 to I-8.

dollars. It combined previously separate funds for child day care services and for training service professionals with unrestricted money for direct service provision. It also removed several eligibility restrictions in the Title XX programs, including a requirement that 50 percent of the *federal* dollars (that is, 50 percent of the 75 percent federal share of expenditures) be spent on recipients of public welfare programs. It eliminated a number of detailed requirements for planning and reporting, as well as certain requirements that had been associated with particular services fundable under Title XX. Most notable was the final removal of proposed regulations establishing standards for child day care known as FIDCR (Federal Interagency Day Care Requirements).[3]

The characteristics of the social services block grant thus suggest several general issues of programmatic and administrative change, which are explored in turn in this chapter:

- Did states choose to sustain their own social services spending when no longer required to do so? Did they in addition replace federal funds or did they take advantage of the elimination of state matching requirements to reduce their own funding?

- How do the state program priorities under the social services block grant compare with program priorities under the previous Title XX programs?

- Has the transition to the social services block grant resulted in specific administrative changes and gains in efficiency?

- How have state and local relations been affected?

- Has the elimination of targeting requirements changed the nature of the population receiving social services?

State Choices: Funding Replacement

Most of the eighteen states in the data sample fully replaced the federal funds cut from the social services block grant, at least when measured in nominal terms. Although all of the states except Florida had to cut spending from federal grant sources, ten of the fourteen states for which fiscal 1984 data were available spent more total funds, from all sources, on social services

---

3. The final postponement of these controversial regulations before elimination, along with a brief summary of their history, is given in *Federal Register*, vol. 46, no. 37 (July 17, 1981), pp. 37049–37501.

in that year than they did in fiscal 1981, even before counting expenditures from the supplement to the Emergency Jobs Appropriations bill. Only six of the fourteen states, however, managed to increase *real* spending on social services as adjusted by the GNP deflator over the period (see tables 7 and 8).

The degree of state replacement of federal funds stands in contrast to early speculation that the states would not replace federal grant funds, especially for programs like social services that were thought to have weak political support. Early studies of the implementation of the block grants seemed to confirm that state governments were not replacing lost social services dollars.

One reason that state replacement was not more visible in the first year after block-grant implementation concerns the timing of implementation in relation to a state's fiscal year. For most states the planning for fiscal 1982 was complete and the state legislature was out of session by the time the block grants were finalized by Congress. State legislatures were forced to deal with block grants earlier in anticipation of what they might include, as both the number of blocks and the programs contained in them were in flux. When the block grants went into effect in October 1981 most states were only months away from beginning the budgeting process for state fiscal 1983. Thus many states made only minimal adjustments until the legislature and the administering agencies could more fully review the state's long-run posture toward the block grants.

Perhaps the best example of this is the state of Texas. The legislature, acting in anticipation of the first year of the block grants, added a series of riders to their appropriations bill, which prohibited state agencies from increasing state funding for services consolidated under the block grants. When the legislature reconvened, it decided to accept potentially controversial blocks such as the community services block grant and approved additional program expansion, particularly in programs providing home- and community-based care for adults. These steps substantially increased state social services spending, beginning in state fiscal 1983.

Delay in implementing policy changes was also a factor in initial implementation. In Michigan, for example, a decision was made to transfer a portion of the financial responsibility for adoption and foster care services to local governments. This had to survive a court test, given Michigan's Headlee Amendment (which limits the amount of expenditure responsibility that the state can shift to the local level), so that the major effects of the state decision were not realized until state fiscal 1983.

TABLE 7

CHANGE IN SOCIAL SERVICES EXPENDITURES, BY SOURCE OF FUNDS, SELECTED STATES,
STATE FISCAL YEARS 1981, 1983, AND 1984
($ Millions)

State	1981		1983				1984			
	Title XX	Total[a]	Social Services Block Grant[c]	Emergency Jobs Appropriations Bill Funds	Total[a] without Jobs Bill Funds	Total with Jobs Bill Funds	Social Services Block Grant[b]	Emergency Jobs Appropriations Bill Funds	Total[a] without Jobs Bill Funds	Total with Jobs Bill Funds
Arizona	32.4	39.8	28.9	0.0	37.1	37.1	31.4	2.9	39.3	42.2
California	304.6	732.3	257.4	0.0	754.0	754.0	260.5	27.0	745.9	772.9
Colorado	36.1	81.8	31.1	0.0	84.4	84.4	35.9	2.3	91.8	94.0
Florida	100.6	154.1	99.6	7.8	158.2	166.1	113.2	0.0	182.5	182.5
Illinois	n.a.	211.7	n.a.	0.0	255.2	255.2	n.a.	13.8	252.6	266.4
Kentucky	45.8	68.4	39.5	1.6	74.8	76.4	40.2	2.3	70.9	73.2
Massachusetts	69.4	149.0	64.8	0.0	164.2	164.2	66.2	4.4	190.3	194.7
Michigan	115.4	580.3	107.9	12.4	578.6	591.0	115.1	0.0	569.3	569.3
Minnesota	53.3	150.9	43.8	3.3	254.4	257.7	47.5	0.0	251.0	251.0
Missouri	45.2	61.3	41.9	0.0	56.3	56.3	n.a.	n.a.	n.a.	n.a.

New Jersey	97.6	149.1	78.7	5.5	149.2	154.7	78.9	0.0	150.8	150.8
New York	235.8	796.2	205.1	13.3	984.8	997.3	206.1	n.a.	983.7	983.7
North Carolina	72.0	100.0	64.3	4.6	92.4	97.0	69.6	0.0	90.3	90.3
Ohio	142.9	187.4	115.5	0.0	155.1	155.1	n.a.	6.4	n.a.	n.a.
Oregon	32.4	60.7	30.8	3.2	67.6	70.6	30.5	0.0	73.4	73.4
Texas	168.9	296.3	156.1	10.8	326.3	337.1	163.1	0.0	325.9	325.9
Vermont	6.4	15.1	5.3	0.4	17.9	18.3	n.a.	0.0	n.a.	n.a.
Virginia	64.9	85.7	57.3	0.0	75.8	75.8	56.9	4.0	75.6	79.6

SOURCES: Based on state fiscal years 1981 and 1983 expenditure data as reported to The Urban Institute and the U.S. General Accounting Office; state fiscal 1984 expenditure data as reported by the states to The Urban Institute.

n.a. Not available.

a. "Total" expenditure figures include spending from the following: Title XX in federal fiscal 1981 and social services block grants in federal fiscal years 1983 and 1984 (including transfers into and out of these block grants), other federal funds (intertitle transfers), state funds, local funds, and other funds (fees, contributions).

b. *After* transfers into (out of) the social services block grant from (to) other block grants.

TABLE 8

PERCENTAGE CHANGE IN SOCIAL SERVICES EXPENDITURES, BY SOURCE OF FUNDS, SELECTED STATES AND PERIODS, STATE FISCAL YEARS 1981–84[a]

State	Percentage Change, Spending from Social Service Block Grant			Percentage Change, Total Spending without Emergency Jobs Appropriations Bill			Percentage Change, Total Spending with Jobs Bill		
	1981–83	1983–84	1981–84	1981–83	1983–84	1981–84	1981–83	1983–84	1981–84
Arizona	−10.8	8.6	−3.1	−6.7	5.9	−1.4	−6.9	13.8	6.0
California	−15.5	1.2	−14.5	3.0	−1.1	−1.9	3.0	2.5	5.6
Colorado	−13.8	15.4	−0.6	3.2	8.8	12.2	3.2	11.4	14.9
Florida	−0.9	13.6	12.6	2.9	15.2	18.6	9.1	8.6	18.6
Illinois	n.a.	n.a.	n.a.	20.5	−1.0	19.3	20.5	4.4	25.8
Kentucky	−13.7	1.8	−12.1	9.3	−5.2	3.6	11.6	−3.8	7.4
Massachusetts	−6.7	2.3	−4.5	10.2	15.9	27.7	10.2	18.6	30.7
Michigan	−6.5	6.7	−0.3	−0.3	n.a.	n.a.	1.5	n.a.	n.a.
Minnesota	−17.9	8.3	−11.0	68.6	−1.3	66.3	70.8	−2.6	66.3
Missouri	−7.3	n.a.	n.a.	−8.2	n.a.	n.a.	−8.2	n.a.	n.a.
New Jersey	−19.3	0.3	−19.2	0.0	1.1	1.1	3.7	2.5	1.1
New York	−13.0	0.5	−12.6	23.6	−0.1	23.5	25.2	−1.4	23.5
North Carolina	−10.7	8.2	−3.3	−7.6	−2.3	−9.7	−7.6	−6.9	−9.7
Ohio	−19.2	n.a.	n.a.	−17.2	n.a.	n.a.	n.a.	n.a.	n.a.
Oregon	−5.2	−0.9	−6.1	11.0	8.6	20.9	16.3	4.0	20.9
Texas	−7.6	4.6	−3.3	10.4	−0.1	10.1	13.8	−3.3	10.0
Vermont	−17.2	n.a.	n.a.	18.2	n.a.	n.a.	n.a.	n.a.	n.a.
Virginia	−11.7	−0.7	−12.3	−11.6	−0.3	−11.8	−11.6	5.4	−7.1

SOURCES: Same as table 7.

n.a. Not available.

a. The total percentage changes for the federal block grant for fiscal years 1981–83 was −10 percent; for fiscal years 1983–84, 0.9 percent; and for fiscal years 1981–84, −9.2 percent.

Sources of Replacement Funds

States had several options in generating replacement funds for social services (see tables 9 and 10).

One possibility was to require or authorize greater local funding support or greater use of fees and service payments. Michigan, Minnesota, and New York all shifted part of the replacement burden to local governments. In Michigan, as noted above, the state required that counties share a greater degree of the child foster care and adoption expenses of the state. In Minnesota, the increased local spending was not a direct result of the block grant. Rather, it reflected an earlier state decision to transfer substantial responsibilities for social services from the state to the counties. Along with this transfer of responsibility, a new local levy was created. The levy, coming into full effect at the time of the block grant, generated significant additional local funds for social services. These local increases completely offset relatively static state spending and the decline in federal block-grant support.

In New York the transfer of responsibility to the local governments was more complex. In part, it reflected a conscious state strategy. The state, for example, transferred low-income home energy assistance block-grant funds (for which the state had supplied no match) into the social services block grant and required local governments to match these funds as they would any other social services block-grant funds. The net effect was to increase the local share of service expenditures. On the other hand, New York City apparently was able to induce additional spending from the state through its own strategic behavior. Liebschutz and others reported on this interaction as follows.

> New York State, under its own Comprehensive Child Welfare Reform Act of 1979, reimburses localities for mandated services when Title XX funds are exhausted. New York City, exercising considerable creativity, was able to capture $16 million from the state in this way. New York City transferred the total cost of day care and services for the elderly, both nonmandated services, into Title XX. This shift of nonmandated services meant that the city had insufficient Title XX funds to provide mandated services. To provide them, New York City used the remainder of its Title XX allocation and then allocated an additional $16 million to such services. By invoking the state funding provisions, all funds spent by New York City in excess of its Title XX allocation were matched equally by the state. By this maneuver the city assured the continuation of both mandated and nonmandated services.[4]

---

4. Sarah F. Liebschutz et al., "How State and Local Responses Confound Federal Policy," paper prepared for delivery at the 1983 Annual Meeting of the American Society for Public Administration, April 16–19, 1983, p. 21.

TABLE 9

CHANGE IN NONBLOCK SPENDING ON SOCIAL SERVICES, SELECTED STATES AND PERIODS, STATE FISCAL YEARS 1981–84
($ MILLIONS)

State	Change, Total Nonblock Spending			Change, Other Federal Sources[a]			Change, State Sources			Change, Local Sources[b]		
	1981–83	1983–84	1981–84	1981–83	1983–84	1981–84	1981–83	1983–84	1981–84	1981–83	1983–84	1981–84
Arizona	0.7	−0.31	0.4	0.0	0.0	0.0	3.3	−0.3	3.0	−2.6	0.0	−2.6
California	53.0	−11.2	41.8	19.1	−32.4	−13.3	32.3	11.7	44.0	1.6	9.5	11.1
Colorado	3.4	2.6	6.0	−4.1	1.2	−2.9	6.8	−4.5	2.3	0.7	5.9	6.6
Florida	5.2	10.5	15.7	4.9	9.1	14.0	0.5	2.1	2.6	−0.2	−0.6	−0.8
Illinois	40.8	n.a.	n.a.	0.0	n.a.	n.a.	40.8	n.a.	n.a.	0.0	n.a.	n.a.
Kentucky	13.9	−4.6	9.3	0.5	−0.02	0.5	13.4	−6.9	6.5	0.0	2.3	2.3
Massachusetts	29.6	24.6	54.2	−0.3	n.a.	n.a.	29.9	n.a.	n.a.	0.0	n.a.	n.a.
Michigan	6.1	...	...	−12.7	...	...	4.0	...	...	14.8	...	...
Minnesota	113.0	−7.1	105.9	0.0	0.0	0.0	14.0	1.9	15.9	99.0	−8.9	90.1
Missouri	−1.6	17.2	15.6	1.0	−1.0	0.0	−2.0	20.0	18.0	−0.6	−1.8	−2.4

New Jersey	17.3	−5.2	12.1	0.0	0.0	0.0	18.5	−0.2	18.0	−1.2	−5.0	−6.2
New York	218.8	−14.6	204.2	69.5	n.a.	n.a.	45.0	n.a.	n.a.	104.3	n.a.	n.a.
North Carolina	0.1	−15.4	−15.3	2.6	−8.9	−6.7	−1.3	−7.0	−8.3	−1.2	0.5	0.3
Ohio	−4.8	n.a.	n.a.	0.0	n.a.	n.a.	0.4	n.a.	n.a.	−5.2	n.a.	n.a.
Oregon	8.4	6.3	12.7	9.3	1.2	10.4	−1.0	−5.0	4.0	0.1	0.2	0.3
Texas	42.9	6.4	49.3	18.1	0.4	18.7	25.7	−12.1	37.7	−0.9	−6.1	−7.0
Vermont	3.7	n.a.	n.a.	0.3	n.a.	n.a.	3.4	n.a.	n.a.	0.0	n.a.	n.a.
Virginia	−1.9	0.2	−2.1	0.0	0.0	0.0	−0.3	0.1	−0.3	−1.6	0.1	−1.8

SOURCE: Same as table 7.

n.a. Not available.

a. Other federal resources consist of intertitle transfers. Intertitle transfers are possible because certain social services may be funded under a variety of federal programs. Included here are Title IV(A) (Aid to Families with Dependent Children, AFDC) funds, Title XIX (Medicaid) funds, and Title IV(B) (child welfare services) funds. Block-to-block transfers made possible in P.L. 97-35 are not included, nor are Emergency Jobs Appropriations bill funds.

b. Local sources include state required local matching funds, fees, and other contributions.

TABLE 10

PERCENTAGE CHANGE IN NONBLOCK SPENDING ON SOCIAL SERVICES, SELECTED STATES AND PERIODS, STATE FISCAL YEARS 1981–84

State	Percentage Change, Total Nonblock Spending			Percentage Change, Other Federal Sources[a]			Percentage Change, State Sources			Percentage Change, Local Sources[b]		
	1981–83	1983–84	1981–84	1981–83	1983–84	1981–84	1981–83	1983–84	1981–84	1981–83	1983–84	1981–84
Arizona	10.2	−3.8	6.0	0.0	0.0	0.0	69.8	−3.8	63.3	−100.0	...	−100.0
California	16.1	−2.2	13.5	176.9	100.0	−99.9	12.9	2.8	16.1	2.4	18.2	20.9
Colorado	16.6	4.9	22.3	1.6	18.8	20.6	30.8	−15.4	10.7	3.5	33.5	38.2
Florida	9.9	18.1	29.8	0.0	0.0	0.0	2.5	4.5	7.1	−9.3	−8.7	−17.2
Illinois	20.5	−1.0	19.3	0.0	...	...	23.6	...	...	0.0	...	...
Kentucky	55.7	−13.1	35.3	20.6	−0.6	19.8	60.3	−21.5	25.9	0.0	0.0	0.0
Massachusetts	24.9	24.7	55.7	−6.8	...	...	29.8	...	...	0.0	...	...
Michigan	1.2	...	...	−9.4	...	...	1.2	...	...	75.4	...	...
Minnesota	115.8	−3.3	108.6	0.0	0.0	0.0	35.8	3.5	40.5	169.2	−5.6	154.0
Missouri	−10.6	119.3	96.1	0.0	0.0	0.0	−15.3	172.2	130.5	−25.0	−100.0	−100.0
New Jersey	36.6	−7.3	26.6	0.0	0.0	0.0	65.5	−0.3	64.9	−4.9	−24.7	−28.4
New York	39.0	−0.3	38.8	28.5	...	...	26.9	...	...	70.0	...	...
North Carolina	0.4	−54.8	−54.6	42.3	−100.0	−100.0	−15.5	−98.4	−98.7	−9.0	4.1	−5.3
Ohio	−15.3	...	...	...	...	...	1.4	...	n.a.	−32.1	...	...
Oregon	29.7	17.2	52.0	263.6	9.1	296.6	−4.1	21.0	16.1	...	157.0	...
Texas	33.6	3.8	38.7	57.6	0.9	59.0	28.9	10.6	42.6	−14.1	−100.0	−100.0
Vermont	44.2	...	...	14.3	...	...	50.7	...	...	...	...	...
Virginia	−11.1	1.1	−10.1	0.0	0.0	0.0	−12.1	3.4	−9.1	−10.9	0.6	−10.3

SOURCE: Same as table 7.

n.a. Not available. These programs were eliminated in 1983 and 1984.

a. Same as table 9.
b. Same as table 9.

In effect, New York City used intertitle transfer to maximize state reimbursement to a local government rather than the more conventional use of this device to maximize federal reimbursement to a state.

Intertitle transfers within federal programs did sustain social services spending in some states. Both Title IV(A) and Title XIX of the federal Social Security Act provide for uncapped federal and state sharing of expenses for Aid to Families with Dependent Children (AFDC) and Medicaid, respectively. Some social services programs qualify for federal funding under both the social services block grant and Title IV(A) or Title XIX. If a state transfers such programs to uncapped federal categorical funding, it can then use the capped social services block-grant funds for other social services. This strategy maximizes total federal aid receipts. The U.S. General Accounting Office, in a review of this phenomenon, concluded that in 1980 fifteen states transferred funding of some social services to Title XIX, eight states made transfers to Title IV(A), and some thirty-one states anticipated making transfers in the state fiscal 1980–81 period.[5] Other commentators cite this as a major way of refinancing and reorganizing human services.[6]

Among the states in the sample, the biggest intertitle transfers in response to block grants occurred in Texas, New York, Florida, Oregon, and Michigan. These are shown as "Other Federal Sources in table 9. (Note that Michigan's new transfers of social services programs into Titles IV(A) and XIX were outweighed by the cutbacks made in other social services programs transferred to these titles, accounting for the reduction in net social services funding from other federal sources.) In Oregon a large share of home care services for elderly and impaired people was transferred from the social services block grant to Title XIX and funded as part of the state's Medicaid program. Intertitle transfers were still not larger in response to the block grants, for the simple reason that many states already had exhausted the transfer possibilities at an earlier date as a response to state budget pressures.

Despite fairly extensive use of intertitle transfer and cost shifting to local governments, the primary means of replacement was the state's own budget. A few states specifically earmarked the savings they obtained from the new federal restrictions on AFDC eligibility for the state social services budget. (When the federal government tightened the rules for AFDC eligibility, it

---

5. U.S. General Accounting Office, *Intertitle Transfers: A Way for States to Increase Federal Funding for Social Services*, Report HRD-81-116 (Washington, D.C.: U.S. Government Printing Office, July 1981).
6. Helen Blank, *Children and Federal Care Cuts: A National Survey of the Impact of Title XX Cuts on State Child Care Systems, 1981–1983* (Washington, D.C.: Children's Defense Fund, 1983).

provided cost savings both for itself and for the states.) Oregon, Florida, and New Jersey chose to use the AFDC savings to fund social services for approximately the same population. Other states simply reallocated their budgets to give greater importance to social services.

As tables 9 and 10 reveal, all except two states in the sample (North Carolina and Virginia) increased the state's own spending between state fiscal years 1981 and 1984 (or state fiscal 1983, if these are the latest data available). Ten states increased state funding in real terms, led by Arizona, New Jersey, Missouri, Texas, and Vermont. The states did not, in all cases, view their increases in social services spending as "caused" by the federal aid cuts or by the reorganization of the federal grant structure. Spending growth in Texas, for example, has its origins in a community care program for elderly people, which state officials viewed as independent of block grants. To a large extent, a state's political cast colored its representation of budget change. New York State's leaders went out of their way to characterize their budget actions as a necessary replacement for a diminished federal role in providing services to the poor. Texas, in contrast, characterized its budget growth as primarily an independent decision not influenced by federal policy.

Use of Emergency Jobs Appropriations Bill Funding

In March 1983, Congress appropriated $4.9 billion for emergency jobs creation and humanitarian aid. The purpose of the Emergency Jobs Appropriations bill was to aid victims of the economic recession, particularly the unemployed. Of the total appropriation, $225 million was earmarked for the social services block-grant program. Congress instructed that these funds were to be used to "expand the availability of day care and other services to unemployed and disadvantaged Americans." As table 11 suggests, although there was variation in how states chose to spend the supplemental social service funds, the states tended to favor day care, employment training programs, and home-based services.

States spread out the expenditure from the Emergency Jobs Appropriations bill funds between state fiscal years 1983 and 1984 rather than inject them quickly into the economy in the form of countercyclical job creation. They did this for several reasons: most funds under the basic social services block-grant allotment are spent in this way; most states have established state procedures, such as legislative authorization requirements and program design requirements, which must be met before funds can be spent; requirements for public hearings and other public input attached to the allocation of social services funds can cause delays; and a state's proposal submission process can cause delays in selecting projects and appropriating funds.

The timing of outlays under the bill closely paralleled that under regular social services programs, indicating that this vehicle was not especially suited to countercyclical policy.

State Program Priorities

The social services block grant is used by states to help fund a large array of different programs. Tables 12–14 identify eight of the largest categories of programs and report changes in the share of total social services spending by each program for fiscal years 1981–84.

The majority of states displayed a similar pattern of program adjustments in response to cutbacks in federal aid. Spending became more concentrated on emergency and protective services, and as a result less attention was given to routine services not affecting individuals' safety. Social services that eliminated the need for more expensive institutionalization also were favored. In the first two years of adjustment, for example, relative spending on child protective services increased in fifteen of the seventeen states for which data were available, and relative spending on adult protective services increased in nine of fourteen states. Relative spending on adoption and foster care rose in eleven of seventeen states. Relative spending fell for child day care (thirteen of eighteen states), information and referral (seven of ten states), training of social services personnel, and "other" services.

By the third year of adjustment, when federal funding for social services had appeared to stabilize, states retreated from some of their initial reallocations of program dollars. Seven of ten states decreased relative spending on adult protective services in fiscal 1983–84, while ten of fifteen increased relative spending on child day care. Day care spending was restored, in part because of political pressure brought by groups lobbying for day care and in part because it was singled out for priority in the Emergency Jobs Appropriations bill legislation.

States often were explicit in establishing their program priorities. New York State, for example, indicated "First priority was assigned to services which respond to life threatening circumstances" and "services which alleviate the need for more restrictive service interventions were assigned the next highest priority."[7] Connecticut, a state not included in the sample, formulated explicit program priorities on the basis of formal negotiations among state officials, local officials, and nonprofit service providers. Highest

7. New York State Department of Social Services, *Consolidated Services Plan for April 1, 1982 to September 30, 1984,* "Executive Summary" p. 3 (Albany, New York: NYSDSS, 1982).

TABLE 11

EMERGENCY JOBS APPROPRIATIONS BILL AND SOCIAL SERVICES BLOCK-GRANT FUNDS AND ACTIVITIES FOR SELECTED STATES,
STATE FISCAL YEARS 1983 AND 1984

State	Major Activities Funded	Year Expended	Funds Allocated ($ Millions)	Employment-Related Activities
Arizona	Indian communities received 18.5 percent of allocation	1983, 1984	2.94	In the employment effort priority was given to displaced workers, particularly the long-term unemployed
	Home-based services (emergency services)			
	Employment, education, and training (private industry councils)			
California	Home-based services (elderly)	1984	27.00	. . .
	Foster care			
	Other services (deaf, county services)			
Colorado	Adoption	1984	2.30	. . .
	Foster care			
Florida	Used most Jobs bill funds as an across-the-board increase for most services	1983, 1984	7.75	Displaced homemakers, delinquent youth jobs program, epileptics job training
	Some funds targeted specifically to employment and training			

State	Services	Year	Percent	Notes
Illinois	Family planning	1984	13.77	Focused on young adult job training and on time-limited employment programs
Kentucky	Day care Employment, education, training	1983, 1984	3.93	Funds for juvenile delinquent job training; in manpower department, for general employment programs
Massachusetts	Day care	1984	4.36	⋯
Michigan	Day care Home-based services (chore) Adult protective Adoption and foster care	1983	12.37	Day care services for employed parents
Minnesota	Money went straight to counties; the counties have authority to determine how funds are spent State provided broad guidelines to focus funds on employment and day care services	1983	3.30	⋯
Missouri	Child protective services Employment, education, and training Day care Other services (mental health, long-term care)	1984	2.60	Some funds for education and job training

TABLE 11 (Continued)

State	Major Activities Funded	Year Expended	Funds Allocated ($ Millions)	Employment-Related Activities
New Jersey	Funds allocated in lump sum to counties	1984	5.54	· · ·
	State-provided guidelines to focus funds on day care			
New York	Day care (employment related)	1983	13.30	All funds for employment related activities
	Employment, education, and training	1984	n.a.	
	Information and referral			
North Carolina	Home-based services (elderly)	1983	4.61	· · ·
	Day care			
	Other services (sickle cell anemia research)			
Ohio	Home-based services	1984, 1985	6.4	Information and referral services and day care were all employment related
	Information and referral (employment related)		n.a.	
	Day care			

State	Services	Year	Amount	Notes
Oregon	Jobs bill funds spent across the board to prevent cuts in service	1983	3.20	. . .
Texas	Day care Education, employment and training (AFDC) Family planning Protective services	1983, 1984	10.84	Major focus of Jobs bill funds on employment services for AFDC recipients
Vermont	Day care	1983, 1984	0.38	AFDC job training
Virginia	One-third for social service to the unemployed; two-thirds spread across the board on all social service programs	1984	4.02	Focus on the emergency needs of the unemployed

SOURCE: Funds allocated from unpublished data, Department of Health and Human Services; remaining information from interviews with officials of state social services departments.

n.a.   Not available.

TABLE 12

PERCENTAGES CHANGE IN TOTAL SOCIAL SERVICES FUNDS ALLOCATED TO ADOPTION AND FOSTER CARE, CHILD DAY CARE, AND EMPLOYMENT, EDUCATION, AND TRAINING, SELECTED STATES, STATE FISCAL YEARS 1981–84[a]

State	Adoption and Foster Care				Child Day Care				Employment, Education, and Training			
	1981	1983	1984	Trend 1981–84	1981	1983	1984	Trend 1981–84	1981	1983	1984	Trend 1981–84
Arizona	14.1	16.2	10.1	Down	16.6	18.3	14.8	Down	8.3	10.2	13.9	Up
California	2.3	2.5	2.4	Up	29.6	30.3	30.3	Up	...	...	n.a.	...
Colorado	31.2	32.9	32.6	Up	21.8	15.2	17.8	Down	...	...	n.a.	...
Florida	5.8	6.7	5.0	Down	16.4	17.6	19.1	Up	2.4	0.5	1.0	Down
Illinois	4.4	3.2	6.1	Up	17.5	12.3	12.0	Down	4.4	3.2	3.6	Down
Kentucky	9.4	14.4	13.2	Up	6.1	6.8	8.3	Up	0.4	0.0	0.0	Down
Massachusetts	21.7	21.6	21.9	Up	27.3	25.4	25.6	Down	0.0	0.0	0.0	...
Michigan	20.0	19.6	n.a.	Down	5.3	2.5	n.a.	Down	1.8	3.6	...	Down
Minnesota	6.6	10.8	10.9	Up	7.2	4.5	4.7	Down	1.5	1.9	2.0	Up
Missouri	n.a.	n.a.	n.a.	n.a.	19.4	15.8	n.a.	Down	...	...	n.a.	...
New Jersey	4.0	5.6	8.0	Up	24.7	23.9	29.4	Up	1.5	1.9	1.3	Down
New York	15.0	13.3	15.0	Even	20.0	17.1	20.3	Up	0.3	0.7	1.0	Up
North Carolina	4.2	7.5	17.2	Up	10.6	11.5	14.2	Up	0.2	0.3	0.1	Down
Ohio	7.0	7.4	n.a.	Up	15.3	12.0	n.a.	Down	6.5	5.1	...	Down
Oregon	25.0	22.0	18.5	Down	2.8	2.1	2.0	Down	...	n.a.	...	...
Texas	5.8	5.1	[b]	Down	14.8	11.3	13.0	Down	4.5	4.6	4.5	Even
Vermont	43.0	60.0	n.a.	Up	12.6	7.8	n.a.	Down	...	n.a.	...	...
Virginia	15.4	27.0	26.6	Up	13.5	9.1	9.3	Down	8.8	6.6	6.5	Down

SOURCE: Same as table 7.

n.a.   Not available. Service is provided, but spending is not separately identified by the state.

a.   Data show the percent share of the total service dollar spent on a particular service.

b.   Adoption and foster care are included in child protective services.

TABLE 13

PERCENTAGE CHANGE IN TOTAL SOCIAL SERVICES FUNDS ALLOCATED TO FAMILY PLANNING, HOME-BASED SERVICES, AND INFORMATION AND REFERRAL, SELECTED STATES, STATE FISCAL YEARS 1981–84[a]

State	Family Planning				Home-Based Services				Information and Referral			
	1981	1983	1984	Trend 1981–84	1981	1983	1984	Trend 1981–84	1981	1983	1984	Trend 1981–84
Arizona	1.1	0.8	0.8	Down	7.5	11.3	9.0	Up	2.3	0.8	0.7	Down
California	4.1	5.0	3.6	Down	35.9	35.0	37.4	Up	n.a.	n.a.	n.a.	...
Colorado	...	n.a.	...	Down	4.9	3.8	1.8	Down	n.a.	n.a.	n.a.	...
Florida	4.1	3.5	3.5	Down	8.8	9.7	1.5	Down	4.9	4.5	2.9	Down
Illinois	1.0	1.2	1.7	Up	9.9	7.2	4.8	Down	0.0	0.0	0.0	...
Kentucky	0.0	0.0	0.0	Down	4.0	4.9	5.9	Up	0.03	0.3	0.3	Up
Massachusetts	0.8	0.8	0.7	Down	10.4	11.8	n.a.	Up	n.a.	n.a.	n.a.	...
Michigan	...	n.a.	...	...	n.a.	n.a.	n.a.	...	n.a.	n.a.	n.a.	...
Minnesota	0.2	0.3	0.2	Even	6.2	3.1	5.8	Down	4.3	2.1	2.0	Down
Missouri	...	n.a.	...	...	n.a.	n.a.	n.a.	...	n.a.	n.a.	n.a.	...
New Jersey	2.3	2.6	3.3	Up	11.4	9.9	5.3	Down	4.9	5.2	0.2	Down
New York	3.5	2.9	3.4	Down	43.6	53.1	37.6	Down	1.3	1.3	2.6	Up
North Carolina	1.0	0.9	n.a.	Down	9.6	6.6	12.5	Up	1.4	1.0	0.0	Down
Ohio	...	n.a.	...	...	8.5	11.4	n.a.	Up	1.9	1.4	0.0	Down
Oregon	...	n.a.	...	...	28.8	33.8	48.1	Up	n.a	n.a.	n.a.	...
Texas	7.4	6.3	7.8	Up	27.6	29.7	29.5	Up	n.a	n.a.	n.a.	Up
Vermont	0.7	0.9	n.a.	Down	3.3	3.9	n.a.	Up	n.a.	n.a.	n.a.	Up
Virginia	5.7	2.2	2.1	Down	11.0	11.4	12.6	Up	1.9	2.8	2.8	Up

SOURCE: Same as table 7.

n.a. Not available. Service is provided, but spending is not separately identified by the state.

a. Same as table 12.

TABLE 14

PERCENTAGE CHANGE IN THE PROPORTION OF TOTAL SOCIAL SERVICES FUNDS ALLOCATED TO PROTECTIVE SERVICES FOR CHILDREN AND FOR ADULTS, SELECTED STATES, FISCAL YEARS 1981–84[a]

State	Protective Services for Children				Protective Services for Adults			
	1981	1983	1984	Trend 1981–84	1981	1983	1984	Trend 1981–84
Arizona	5.0	8.6	6.8	Up	3.0	4.0	3.2	Up
California	...	...	n.a.	...	...	...	n.a.	...
Colorado	31.7	36.7	35.6	Up	3.4	4.2	3.5	Up
Florida	16.3	18.9	18.3	Up	7.7	6.9	6.7	Down
Illinois	3.1	5.3	4.2	Up	1.1	0.0	0.0	Down
Kentucky	7.9	18.1	17.4	Up	3.6	6.8	6.3	Up
Massachusetts	13.4	13.0	12.4	Down	...	...	n.a.	...
Michigan	3.4	4.5	n.a.	Up	0.3	0.4	...	Up
Minnesota	8.3	5.2	5.9	Down	1.4	0.7	0.6	Down
Missouri	n.a.	...	...	...	n.a.	n.a.	5.9	Down
New Jersey	7.9	10.7	13.6	Up	1.3	2.8	0.0	Down
New York	6.6	5.4	8.3	Up	1.5	1.5	1.8	Up
North Carolina	3.5	6.5	7.8	Up	0.7	1.4	1.9	Up
Ohio	6.1	9.9	n.a.	Up	2.2	3.1	...	Up
Oregon	10.2	10.4	11.2	Up	...	...	n.a.	...
Texas	18.1	22.5	25.5	Up	7.5	8.5	6.5	Down
Vermont	2.6	3.4	n.a.	Up	7.9	4.5	...	Down
Virginia	9.8	14.4	14.9	Up	1.3	2.8	3.2	Up

SOURCE: Same as table 7.

n.a. Not available. Service is provided, but spending is not separately identified by the state.

a. Same as table 12.

priority was assigned to adoption and protection services, next priority to employability and family planning, and low priority to counseling, residential treatment, and information and referral.[8] Whatever their eventual allocation priorities, few states employed "across-the-board" budget-cutting strategies for adjusting service dollar shares. Only California might be viewed as using a "pro-rata" strategy for allocating its service dollars. In all other states program adjustment was largely the rule.

Administrative Changes as a Result of the Block Grant

One of the expectations of those favoring block grants was that administrative efficiency could be improved through greater state control. This may not have been a reasonable goal for the social services block grant in particular. Title XX was, in large measure, a block grant before the creation of the social services block grant in fiscal 1982. The fact that relatively little administrative change from the previous program was necessary might suggest that gains in administrative efficiency would be modest. This was in fact borne out in the eighteen states examined. Thirteen of these states reported only minimal administrative changes. The primary changes resulted from the deletion of the social services reporting requirements. In a number of instances the loss of the federal reporting system meant a decrease in the amount of information available to the state. In other cases, such as Florida and Minnesota, state officials claimed that a largely redundant information apparatus was eliminated—one that paralleled a similar automated state system.[9]

Five of the eighteen states, however, reported more significant administrative changes. Illinois, North Carolina, New Jersey, Florida, and Missouri reported that significant savings had accrued as a result of eliminating the complex Title XX eligibility process. Florida claimed a total administrative savings of nearly $4.8 million compared to a total reduction in Title XX funds of some $16 million. Five-sixths of the planning staff was eliminated in Florida. Illinois claimed a reduction in its planning and eligibility determination staff from eighty-nine to twelve. Missouri claimed $3 million in savings from streamlining the eligibility process and reducing state staff from sixty to forty-seven people.

---

8. See State of Connecticut, *A Negotiated Investment Strategy: A Joint Agreement on Principles, Priorities, Allocation and Plans for the Social Services Block Grant* (Hartford, 1983); and Eugene C. Durman, "The Role of the Legislature in Connecticut's Negotiated Investment Strategy," working paper (Washington, D.C.: The Urban Institute, July 1985).

9. Florida Advisory Council on Intergovernmental Relations, *Florida's Implementation of the Federal Block Grants* (Tallahassee, Florida: FACRR, 1982).

It is clear that some states used the relaxed eligibility rules of the social services block grant to revamp their eligibility determination process. This does not necessarily imply a shift away from a low-income, high-need service population. The general trend in the states was to try to tighten eligibility standards, that is, to serve a relatively poorer or "needier" population (see below) at the same time that they substituted neighborhood-wide eligibility for case-by-case determination of individual eligibility.

Probably the most important "efficiency" gain uncovered in the study lies at the margin of efficiency and program quality. This concerns the change in child day care standards. Day care provided under the Title XX program was to be subject in federal fiscal 1982 to the Federal Interagency Day Care Requirements (FIDCR). These highly controversial rules governing staffing ratios and other aspects of day care oversight had been debated for years and, although they had repeatedly been delayed by Congress, were scheduled to go into effect in federal fiscal 1982. With the creation of the social services block grant, the FIDCR were dropped. States as diverse as Texas and Illinois claimed major savings as a result of not having to implement the FIDCR. These states incorporated FIDCR or similar requirements into state regulations in anticipation of their implementation in October 1982 and were required by Title XX regulations to hold to them.

States realized their savings principally by allowing day care centers to decrease the ratio of children to staff below that required under the FIDCR. This change brought with it the "quality" issue—there are now more children per staff member in a given day care center and less formally trained care givers. Advocates of the change point both to the cost savings and to the potentially large gains in the number of individuals served. Expenditures for day care in Texas, for example, declined from $36.6 million in state fiscal 1981 to $29.5 million in state fiscal 1982 At the same time, however, the number of full-time equivalent slots available for children increased from 12,000 to nearly 14,000. Although various factors were associated with the decline in the average daily rate of reimbursement paid to day care centers, Texas officials ascribed the majority of the change to reduced standards resulting from the eliminated federal requirements. Illinois officials estimated that care not regulated by the FIDCR was 10 to 20 percent less expensive than care provided under FIDCR.

The quality-quantity issue arises in a slightly different way in Michigan and other states that switched day care funding to the AFDC program to take advantage of Title IV(A)'s open-ended matching. Institutionally, the effect of this transfer is to place dollars that formerly went directly to day care centers in the hands of recipients who could then choose among several day care options available to them. A Michigan Department of Social Services study found that a number of recipients were using less expensive forms of care (friends, relatives not living in the home, and so on) as substitutes for more expensive center-based day care. The analyst summarized the results as follows:

> The composition of care has changed dramatically from April '81 to April '82, the most significant event being the decline of center utilization and a corresponding increase in day care home placement. Most of this change can be attributed to the environment in which employment related day care is used. In general the cost containment measures . . . have tended to favor day care home and in home care at the expense of the day care centers.[10]

In general, the day care situation suggests that states, particularly those under financial pressure, are willing to look for less expensive forms of care and that cost savings per child may help cushion the loss of funding, although at the expense of traditional measures of service quality.

State and Local Relations under the Block Grant

The social services block grant permitted rather than required change in relations between state and local governments. Fourteen of the eighteen states examined did not note any significant change. Four states did claim that they experienced such change. In these states (Illinois, New Jersey, California, North Carolina) efforts have been under way to increase the role of local governments, or to reduce the administrative burden placed on local governments by the state.

One common attribute of these states was the fact that each had a state supervised and locally administered social service system rather than the more common state administered system. This tradition of local control appeared to facilitate a shift toward greater local autonomy. California created, in effect, a miniblock to county governments and greatly reduced the number of state mandates imposed upon counties. New Jersey strengthened the role of local advisory committees: the state provided them a much more complete look at all the funding received by local nonprofit agencies, thereby enabling those local committees to make more comprehensive allocation decisions. North Carolina has reduced to a large extent the administrative burden on local governments. The governor's task force in Illinois has proposed a large-scale restructuring of the service delivery system. One major thrust of the Illinois

---

10. Stephen J. Smucker, "Cost of Day Care in FY 1982: Savings of the Transfer to IV-A," (Lansing, Michigan: Department of Social Services, Office of Planning, Budget and Evaluation, May 1982).

effort would be to simplify the funds allocation process to county and nonprofit organizations.[11]

Although the existence of a state-supervised and locally administered system was important, the change in state-local relations accompanying the block grant owed much to the institutional circumstances in the individual states. In Minnesota, for example, the block grant was overshadowed by far more comprehensive state legislation. Under the Community Social Service Act, which predated the social services block grant, Minnesota's system of services was essentially converted into a block grant from the state to the local government. The federal block grant could do little in addition to encourage that process.

Another issue that was pivotal for state-local relations emerged in about a quarter of the states (Florida, New Jersey, Minnesota, and California). This was a concern about geographic equity, the "fair" distribution of resources to all areas within the state. Only in Minnesota could the block grant per se be characterized as a major precipitating factor in the concern about equity. The concerns had long existed in other states, and the block grant provided one additional context for ongoing debate. In Minnesota the issue arose primarily because of the funding reduction associated with the block grant. The state, in an effort to be fair to counties that had in the past received a larger share of state and federal dollars than population alone would dictate, developed a compromise formula. This formula "held harmless" existing grantees by guaranteeing them their historical levels of funding, but allocated new resources on the basis of factors that would eventually ensure greater geographic equity. The formula does not have the desired effect, however, if resources have been decreased rather than increased. As funding reductions under block grants became apparent, various Minnesota counties expressed concern that there was little or no progress toward achieving greater geographic equity.

The issue surfaced most visibly and with the greatest political involvement in New Jersey. There the central concern was the formula for distributing state and federal service dollars to the localities. Counties in the southern tier of New Jersey felt strongly that they had not received adequate resources in the past. They argued for a revision in the formula that would provide them a "fairer" share of the total resources. Other counties, quite naturally, opposed this revision and proposed an alternative that would actually increase their share of the resources. The state department eventually proposed a compromise that temporarily defused the issue.

---

11. Governor's Task Force on Block Grant Implementation, *Final Report* (Springfield, Illinois: Governor's Task Force, 1983).

Elimination of Targeting Requirements

How did the slower growth, or cutbacks, in states' social services spending, coupled with relaxation of federal eligibility rules, affect the population receiving social services? Table 15 summarizes some of the major changes in eligibility noted by state officials during interviews.[12]

The trends shown in table 15 are fairly clear. Eleven states either increased fees for selected services or decreased the income eligibility level for these services. Both responses served to target net program benefits to the poorest households. Day care was specifically singled out for changes in eligibility in nine states. No state indicated a movement in the opposite direction, that is, to increase the income eligibility level for services, although Virginia did limit the proportion of a day care center's population that could be from AFDC families. Five states made eligibility changes in home-care services that could have negative effects on the elderly. In each case, services became more restricted to those "in greatest need," typically defined as those requiring in-home services to prevent entry into a nursing home.

Where formal eligibility rules for individual programs were changed, they served to focus program benefits more closely on the lowest income households. Working households found themselves displaced from eligibility for some programs, especially day care. There also was a widespread shift from income level to other, qualitative measures of need in establishing program eligibility. The appendix to this chapter describes in detail the program and eligibility shifts in one state, Virginia. As in many other states, removal of the federal requirement that 50 percent of recipients be participants in AFDC, Medicaid, or other federal categorical programs greatly increased the share of social service recipients who were served without regard to income because they needed family protection or were otherwise at risk.

---

12. The table focuses on program adjustments that affect recipients differentially by income, demographic, or public assistance status. The changes should be placed in the context of the "dual" eligibility system required under the federal Title XX program. Federal regulations required that at least half of the federal dollars be spent on public assistance recipients—such as the recipients of AFDC or Supplemental Security Income (SSI). In addition to these "categorically eligible" clients, states were to receive federal reimbursement for "income eligible" people (those at or below 80 percent of the state's median income). At a state's option the eligibility level could be set below the 80 percent figure (at 70 to 60 percent of the state median income). In addition, a state could receive federal reimbursement for services extended up to 115 percent of the state median income so long as the state imposed a sliding fee schedule on those between 80 and 115 percent of the median.

TABLE 15

CHANGE IN ELIGIBILITY FOR SOCIAL SERVICES, SELECTED STATES

State	Eligibility Changes
Arizona	Tightened eligibility for in-home care services to serve primarily those with severe impairments revealed in a formal needs assessment Increased payments required under sliding fee schedule for day care
California	State established guidelines for county department to reduce in-home social service, including eliminating eligibility to those who in the absence of services would not require out-of-home medical placement
Colorado	No longer used social services block-grant funds for developmentally disabled recipients served by community boards Reduced income eligibility for day care from 65 to 57 percent of the state median family income
Florida	Eliminated the local services program for the elderly; largely replaced the funding with Older Americans Act and state funds
Illinois	Lowered income eligibility in day care from 80 to 70 percent of state median income
Kentucky	Reduced eligibility for day care from 80 to 60 percent of state median family income
Massachusetts	No eligibility changes Increased sliding fee schedule for day care, although not because of federal cuts as the state increased its funding
Michigan	No change in department of social services policy, which had in the past spent between 55 and 60 percent of Title XX for participants in federal categorical programs
Minnesota	Eligibility determined by counties; no evidence of shift away from AFDC population
Missouri	Required 50 cent per day copayment for vendor day care First restricted eligibility for day care, then relaxed these restrictions as day care spending fell below projected levels
New Jersey	Federal eligibility requirements for Title XX services were eliminated, but the state chose to retain existing levels for state fiscal year 1983
New York	Imposed required $23 fee for second child for day care per month Increased maximum monthly fee for child in day care from $40 to $45

TABLE 15   (*Continued*)

State	Eligibility Changes
New York (*continued*)	Lowered income levels at which fees for day care are charged; for a family of two, income eligibility decreased from $7,760 to $6,220 Lowered maximum income eligibility for day care for families of four or more from 100 to 94 percent of state's median income
North Carolina	No specific eligibility changes, although "nonmandated" services were reduced
Ohio	Increased fee schedule for all services except those provided without regard to income
Oregon	Restricted eligibility for in-home services to those at high or moderate risk of institutionalization
Texas	Restricted eligibility for protective services to those experiencing abuse or neglect; services to those "at risk" limited to initial investigation and referral to community agency Day care restricted primarily to AFDC recipients or those needing it as a protective service Required fee schedule for provider facility day care Family planning priorities established to emphasize services to recipients of AFDC, refugee cash assistance, and SSI Community care rules modified to delete the lowest priority levels for service
Vermont	Increased fee schedule for day care services. Families of three or less eligible for free day care only if gross monthly income is below $450 (up from $400) At higher income levels, a family was required to pay a larger percentage of the total cost
Virginia	Developed optional fee schedule for localities Restricted day care for children of AFDC recipients

SOURCE: State plans for social services block-grant expenditures and interviews with state officials.

Appendix

Virginia's Response to the Social Services Block Grant

A number of states have replaced lost social services block-grant dollars with other federal, state, or local resources, but this has not been the case for Virginia. Virginia's response has been to translate lost dollars into service reductions. The state did not replace federal dollars with local or state funds, nor has it sought additional sources of federal funding. Thus Virginia's decisions concerning program priorities are a useful example of how particular recipient groups and services fare under conditions of fiscal retrenchment.

Although states are no longer required to report to the federal government using the social services reporting requirements system, Virginia has continued to maintain its data on recipients in the system. The availability of this data in Virginia permits examination, albeit limited, of the targeting issues of concern in block-grant evaluations.

Table 16 shows recipient distribution before and after the block grant. The "categorically eligible" group refers to those who receive public aid, such as AFDC and Supplemental Security Income recipients (excluding the blind for whom data were unavailable), Medicaid recipients, participants in the Work Incentive Program, and Child Welfare Service recipients. The "income eligible" group is a rough proxy for the "working poor"—those whose income falls below 80 percent of the state median family income but are not recipients of public aid from the above-mentioned programs. The third category consists of those who receive services "without regard to income." This is, at best, a crude proxy for "nonpoor." Recipients in this category are not necessarily better off than those in the first two categories. Rather, the state does not conduct a "means" test to determine recipients' eligibility for this last category. In Virginia, for example, recipients are provided family planning services, child protective services, and adult protective services without checking on their income status. In certain instances, recipients of child protective or other services are identified as categorically eligible or income eligible typically because they or their families have been so identified based on other service requests.

Given the information available two major questions emerge. Has a shift occurred in the service dollar away from "income maintenance" recipients as a result of eliminating the requirement that 50 percent of federal funds go to such recipients? Is there an increasing tendency to serve the "nonpoor" with scarce social service dollars? Operationally, the answer to the first question is yes if the proportion of dollars spent on categorically eligible clients declined disproportionately to other groups. The second question would receive an affirmative response if expenditures without regard to income increased because additional kinds of services were provided without any eligibility determination. In Virginia, for example, a decision to offer day care or adult home services without regard to income would suggest a probable diversion of service dollars away from the poor, because both services previously required a determination of income, public assistance status, or both.

Although overall spending on social services has declined, the data in table 16 suggest that Virginia has not used a strategy of pro-rata reductions to allocate spending cuts. Spending on income eligibles declined more than 30 percent in the two-year period, while spending on categorically eligible recipients declined less, a little more than 19 percent. In contrast, spending on recipients in the category "without regard to income" rose more than 8 percent between state fiscal 1981 and state fiscal 1983. This exactly reverses state fiscal 1980–81 trends in which Virginia increased spending on income-eligible recipients by 9 percent and on the categorically eligible by 8.4 percent while decreasing expenditures on recipients served without regard to income by 9.5 percent.

These results should not be interpreted as shifting resources away from the "needy" within service categories. As table 16 indicates, nearly all the changes result from priority setting among types of *service* rather than among types of recipients directly. Virginia has assigned a relatively low priority to child day care, home-based services, and employment and training services, none of which were or became available without regard to income. Among services that are offered to recipients "without regard to income" and to those on an "income-determined" basis, adoption and foster care and family planning were *less* substantially reduced for income determined recipients than for the others. The entire increase in spending on recipients without regard to income reflects a strong priority assigned to protective services to both children and adults in danger of abuse or neglect. These services were the only ones on which spending was increased, not only in total but within each eligibility category.

Spending for protective services is clearly compatible with federal priorities. "Protection" was explicitly included as one of four primary goals of the Title XX program, and language retaining this emphasis was included in

TABLE 16

VIRGINIA'S SOCIAL SERVICES SPENDING TRENDS, FISCAL YEARS 1980, 1981, AND 1983

(Thousands of Dollars unless Otherwise Indicated)

Income Category and Year or Period[a]	Adoption and Foster Care	Child Day Care	Employment, Education, and Training	Family Planning	Home-Based Services	Protective Services		All Other Services	Total Services for Year or Period
						Child	Adult		
Income eligible									
1980	1,985	2,950	2,852	955	1,282	489	93	9,092	19,699
1981	2,411	2,975	3,568	1,303	1,396	483	92	9,252	21,480
1983	1,997	830	2,335	440	783	561	141	7,889	14,976
Percentage change									
1980–81	21.4	0.8	25.1	36.4	8.9	−1.1	−0.9	1.8	9.0
1981–83	−17.1	−72.1	−34.6	−66.2	−43.9	16.1	53.3	−14.7	−30.3
Without regard to income									
1980	251	0.0	0.0	2,865	0.0	7,143	733	1,224	12,216
1981	142	0.0	0.0	2,940	0.0	6,077	919	984	11,061
1983	82	0.0	0.0	308	0.0	9,298	1,334	969	11,990
Percentage change									
1980–81	−43.5	...	...	2.6	...	−14.9	25.3	−19.7	−9.5
1981–83	−41.8	...	...	−89.5	...	53.0	45.2	−1.5	8.4

Categorically eligible									
1980	10,248	8,921	3,958	796	9,792	1,467	212	21,257	56,652
1981	10,543	10,151	4,401	934	8,383	1,648	191	25,165	61,416
1983	10,000	6,410	2,635	677	5,383	2,084	312	22,133	49,635
Percentage change									
1980–81	2.9	13.8	11.2	17.3	−14.4	12.3	−10.0	−18.4	8.4
1981–83	−5.2	−36.9	−40.1	−27.5	−35.8	26.4	63.6	−12.1	−19.2
Total, all categories									
1980	12,484	11,871	6,810	4,617	11,074	9,099	1,038	31,573	88,567
1981	13,096	13,127	7,968	5,177	9,778	8,208	1,202	35,400	93,956
1983	12,080	7,240	4,970	1,425	6,167	11,942	1,787	30,991	76,602
Percentage change									
1980–81	4.9	10.6	17.0	12.1	−11.7	−9.8	−15.8	−12.1	6.1
1981–83	−7.8	−44.8	−37.6	−72.5	−36.9	45.5	48.7	−12.5	−18.5

SOURCE: State of Virginia, Department of Social Services, unpublished data for the years shown.

a. See text discussion for definitions of the terms *income eligible, without regard to income,* and *categorically eligible.*

the Omnibus Budget Reconciliation Act. Federal legislation requiring professionals to report incidents of abuse are further evidence of national concern. However, to the extent that reported child abuse and the need for assistance affect all strata of the population, Virginia's priority assigned to these services probably means that fewer dollars are being spent on the AFDC population as a group. Similar observations could be made of other states that dramatically increase relative spending on protective services.

Table 17 focuses directly on the effects of spending reductions on recipients. The data suggest that, in Virginia at least, and in contrast to reports from administrators in some other states, spending reductions greatly affected the number of clients served. Overall, an 18.5 percent reduction in spending was accompanied by a reduction in recipients of nearly 34 percent. By far the largest number of recipients were affected by reductions in family planning and in "other services." The former program served over 40,000 fewer people; all other services served over 50,000 fewer people. Spending reductions in other programs affected fewer persons, but a high percentage of those previously served. Child day care recipients and recipients of employment services, for example, were reduced by more than half.

Consistent with spending trends, the number of protective services recipients increased over this period (child protection, 7 percent; adult protection, 28 percent). It seems fair to state that decision-making in Virginia substantially shifted the target groups for service dollars. Healthy but poor families requiring day care, employment, and family planning services were assigned a lower priority, while those vulnerable to abuse, either young or old, were assigned a higher priority. The "needy" are clearly being served both before and after the creation of the block grant, but the mix of needs is being addressed differently.

TABLE 17

RECIPIENTS SERVED IN VIRGINIA, BY SERVICE AND INCOME CATEGORY, FISCAL YEARS 1980, 1981, AND 1983
(Thousands of Dollars unless Otherwise Indicated)

Income Category and Year or Period[a]	Adoption and Foster Care	Child Day Care	Employment, Education, and Training	Family Planning	Home-Based Services	Protective Services		All Other Services	Total Services for Year or Period
						Child	Adult		
Income eligible									
1980	4,785	2,834	5,008	51,623	1,434	2,688	544	40,214	109,130
1981	4,377	2,747	5,788	59,316	1,384	2,620	510	41,833	118,575
1983	3,612	731	2,653	27,058	1,298	2,349	598	30,292	68,591
Percentage change									
1980–81	−8.5	−3.1	15.6	14.9	−3.5	−2.5	−6.3	4.0	8.7
1981–83	−17.5	−73.4	−54.2	−54.4	−6.2	−10.3	17.3	−27.6	−42.2
Without regard to income									
1980	751	0.0	0.0	11,737	0.0	21,524	2,114	3,761	39,887
1981	397	0.0	0.0	10,624	0.0	20,852	2,557	2,761	37,191
1983	214	0.0	0.0	4,181	0.0	23,774	3,427	2,513	34,109
Percentage change									
1980–81	−47.1	0.0	0.0	−9.5	0.0	−3.1	21.0	−26.6	−6.8
1981–83	−46.1	0.0	0.0	−60.6	0.0	14.0	34.0	9.0	−8.3

TABLE 17 (Continued)

Income Category and Year or Period[a]	Adoption and Foster Care	Child Day Care	Employment, Education, and Training	Family Planning	Home-Based Services	Protective Services		All Other Services	Total Services for Year or Period
						Child	Adult		
Categorically eligible									
1980	16,392	10,810	14,094	4,404	9,084	8,493	1,038	108,031	172,346
1981	13,086	13,587	14,632	4,847	8,582	8,686	830	118,627	182,877
1983	11,806	6,939	7,059	2,359	5,703	8,288	958	78,258	121,370
Percentage change									
1980–81	−20.2	25.7	3.8	10.1	−5.5	2.3	−20.0	9.8	6.1
1981–83	−9.8	−48.9	−51.8	−51.3	−33.5	−4.6	15.4	−34.0	−33.6
Total, all categories									
1980	21,928	13,644	19,102	67,764	10,518	32,705	3,696	152,006	321,363
1981	17,860	16,334	20,420	74,787	9,966	32,158	3,897	163,221	338,643
1983	15,632	7,670	9,712	33,598	7,001	34,411	4,983	111,063	224,070
Percentage change									
1980–81	−18.6	19.7	6.9	10.4	−5.2	−1.7	5.4	7.4	5.4
1981–83	−12.5	−53.0	−52.4	−55.1	−29.8	7.0	27.9	32.0	33.8

SOURCE: Same as table 16.

a. Same as table 16.

CHAPTER 3

COMMUNITY SERVICES

The community services block grant is an excellent example of the compromise fashioned between the Reagan administration and Congress in developing block grants. On the one hand, the community services block grant transferred control of funding of the Community Action Agencies from the federal government to the state governments. Thus a network of local agencies that had been created, at least in part, to challenge state and local governments was to be controlled and funded by one of those levels of government. The block grant made clear that the states were to determine how the funds were used, that the states were to determine program priorities within broad outlines stipulated, and that low-income populations were to be targeted, but it designated no specific subsets of the low-income population for services.

On the other hand, the block grant also contained a stringent earmarking requirement added by Congress explicitly to limit the states' ability to exercise what a majority in Congress feared might be an arbitrary exercise of cutting back or eliminating Community Action Agencies in particular localities. This earmarking requirement—originally intended to apply only to fiscal 1982—guaranteed that 90 percent of the community services block grant funds would go to "eligible entities," primarily Community Action Agencies. The administrative component of spending was to be limited to no more than 5 percent of the total, and 5 percent was to be available to the state to use as it chose. In subsequent negotiations over the community services block grant, Congress retained the stipulation for fiscal 1983 and fiscal 1984 as well. Thus, while the overall thrust of the block grant was to shift a major new administrative and programmatic responsibility to state governments, the 90 percent earmark sharply limited the scope of this state discretion and guaranteed that the primary recipients of the community services block-grant would be the entities funded in 1981 by the Community Services Administration.

Previous Community Services Programs

The programs consolidated into the community services block grant had their origins in the Johnson administration's War on Poverty. The Community Action Agencies, through which the programs were administered, were originally intended to provide a combination of services to and advocacy for impoverished local populations.[1]

Over time, the nature of the Community Action Agencies often changed. A number of them became affiliated with local units of government. Others remained independent but shifted the focus of their activities from advocacy to local service delivery.

The services that could be offered were diverse. The Community Action Agencies often became a conduit for other federal programs designed to reach local populations. Thus, for example, a local Community Action Agency might become the umbrella agency for a Head Start program, a weatherization program, or an emergency fuel program. In a number of instances the Community Action Agencies were either Area Agencies on Aging or were designated by those Area Agencies on Aging to provide services to the elderly in the Community Action Agency target area. A number of these Community Action Agencies offered meals and other food programs to elderly and low-income citizens in their area. With this diversification of services and focus on service provision, many Community Action Agencies became significant actors in the local communities. A state official in Minnesota noted, for example, that in a number of Minnesota counties the Community Action Agency spent more money and provided more services than did the local welfare department. These developments suggest that the Community Action Agencies, created in controversy with an emphasis on advocacy, had over the years become important service-providing entities at the local level, yet were typically independent of both state and local governments.

The now defunct federal Community Services Administration had funded directly a number of these Community Action Agencies in each of the states around the country. Funding was based both on the local incidence of poverty relative to the nation as a whole and on the historical level of funding the agency had received, that is, an agency was seldom cut from year to year,

1. Institute for Local Self Government, *The Challenge of Block Grants: The States Implement the CSBG*, Social Policy Series 4 (Berkeley, California: February 1982).

and funding typically increased slightly to maintain its ability to provide the same level of services. Although there were many agencies in a typical state, there was no attempt by federal officials to be comprehensive in coverage of a given state, and funding for these agencies was not based on the incidence of poverty within the state. Both these facts, the lack of comprehensiveness and the fact that while poverty was the basis of funding it was local income relative to national income that was used to measure poverty, became significant with the creation of the block grant.

State versus Federal Priorities

As mentioned in the beginning of this chapter, the 90 percent earmark to existing grantees sharply limited what otherwise might have been a significant opportunity for state governments to exercise differing priorities from the federal government. Because of this earmarking requirement, the issue of state versus federal priorities becomes in essence several related questions:

- Did states replace federal funding in the community services block grant?

- Were states satisfied with the distribution of block-grant resources within the existing list of grantees? With the geographic distribution of these resources? With the specific entities receiving the funds?

- To what extent did states try to add new organizations as service deliverers under the block grant?

The answers to these questions are clear for the eighteen states of this study. Essentially no replacement of federal with state dollars has occurred in the community services block grant. The states were almost universally dissatisfied with the historical allocation of resources among eligible entities; and almost all states have taken steps to change this allocation. The states are, in addition, concerned about the geographic distribution of community services block-grant funds. All have made efforts to improve within-state geographic equity. States have been apparently far less dissatisfied with Community Action Agencies and other eligible entities as recipients of funds, although in a notable minority of states the issue has arisen of who should be the ultimate recipient for community services block-grant funds. The remainder of this chapter elaborates on each of these observations for the eighteen states in the sample.

State Replacement of Funds

The issue of state replacement of federal community services block-grant dollars is highlighted in tables 18 and 19. The tables focus on the extent of federal and state contributions to the local Community Action Agencies.[2] Many of the eighteen states in the sample experienced a 20 percent or more reduction in federal community services block-grant funds between fiscal years 1981 and 1983 or 1981 and 1984, after inclusion of funding from the Emergency Jobs Appropriations bill. This was matched by a similar reduction in the total of federal and state funding. Overall, in contrast to the situation in the social services block grant, replacement of federal funds with state funds was either zero or negative, that is, the states often spent slightly less of their own funds than they had before the creation of the block grant. Nine of eighteen states cut their own budget support, while only Florida increased it.

The modest negative replacement resulted from several factors. First, most states received a state grant from the Office of Economic Opportunity in fiscal 1981, which required a 50 percent state match. With the advent of the community services block grant, states could claim up to 5 percent of the block grant for administrative purposes, with no required match. Most states, in fact, claimed the 5 percent or a portion of it and reduced or eliminated the state match that had been formerly required. States with zero replacement were those without a federal grant requiring a match in state fiscal 1981.

Michigan and Minnesota were unique among the states in the sample; they allocated a significant amount of state funds to the community action programs before the creation of the block grant. Both these states responded to the overall fiscal difficulties at the state level by cutting back modestly on their state contributions to the Community Action Agencies, which is reflected as negative replacement in tables 18 and 19.

---

2. Local funding for the Community Action Agencies is excluded for several reasons. It was difficult for most states to provide accurate reporting on local spending because these community agencies typically are not under state control. A number of states required the local agencies to continue to provide matching funds in cash or in kind, but could provide no information about whether the agency, in fact, maintained its original level of spending or reduced spending and contributions to a level commensurate with that required for match of a smaller grant. No complete information is available on the extent to which local agencies, given the need to absorb a particular change, were able to do so from their own resources. Scattered evidence suggests, however, that to a large extent the local agencies were not able to replace these lost funds. The budgets of the local agencies are comprised of a variety of sources in addition to federal block-grant and state funds; thus, the total impact on a given local Community Action Agency would be the net effect of changes in Older Americans Act programs, Head Start programs, energy programs, plus the many local programs administered through the Community Action Agency.

TABLE 18

CHANGE IN COMMUNITY SERVICES BLOCK-GRANT EXPENDITURES FOR SELECTED STATES,
STATE FISCAL YEARS 1981, 1983, AND 1984
(Millions of Dollars)

State	1981		1983			1984		
	Federal	Total	Federal	Total	Total including Jobs Bill Funds	Federal	Total	Total including Jobs Bill Funds
Arizona	3.6	3.7	2.7	2.7	2.9	2.7	2.7	2.7
California	38.4	38.6	29.2	29.2	29.2	27.9	27.9	n.a.
Colorado	4.2	4.2	2.9a	2.9	3.1	2.9	2.9	2.9
Florida	11.6	11.7	9.6	10.9	11.5	9.7	10.5	10.5
Illinois	19.3	19.3	15.6	15.6	17.0	14.6	14.6	14.6
Kentucky	7.1	7.1	5.6	5.6	6.0	5.6	5.6	6.1
Massachusetts	11.5	11.6	8.6	8.6	8.6	8.2	8.2	10.7
Michigan	15.7	17.2	12.0	13.0	14.2	12.4	13.5	13.5
Minnesota	5.7	7.1	3.9b	4.9	5.2	4.0	5.3	5.3
Missouri	9.3	9.3	8.4	8.4	8.9	9.8	9.8	9.8
New Jersey	10.9	10.9	9.0	9.0	9.6	8.6	8.6	8.6
New York	34.1	34.3	28.6	28.7	30.2	27.1	27.1	27.1
North Carolina	12.7	12.8	8.4	8.4	8.9	8.7	8.7	8.7
Ohio	17.1	17.1	12.8	12.8	14.1	12.8	12.8	12.8
Oregon	4.1	4.1	2.8	2.8	3.1	2.8	2.8	2.8
Texas	20.1	20.2	15.8	15.8	16.8	15.8	15.8	15.8
Vermont	1.3	1.3	1.1	1.1	1.1	1.1	1.1	1.2
Virginia	8.4	8.6	5.4	5.4	5.4	5.4	5.4	5.8

SOURCE: Same as table 7.

n.a.   Not available.

a.   Excludes $262,000 transferred to the low-income home energy assistance block grant.

b.   Excludes $1,000,000 transferred to the low-income home energy assistance block grant.

TABLE 19

PERCENTAGE CHANGE IN COMMUNITY SERVICES BLOCK-GRANT EXPENDITURES, SELECTED STATES AND PERIODS, STATE FISCAL YEARS 1981–84

State	Percentage Change, 1981–83 Spending			Percentage Change, 1983–84 Spending			Percentage Change, 1981–84 Spending		
	Federal	Total	Total Including Jobs Bill	Federal	Total	Total Including Jobs Bill	Federal	Total	Total Including Jobs Bill
Arizona	-25.0	-27.0	-21.6	0.0	0.0	-5.9	-25.0	-27.0	-26.2
California	-23.9	-24.3	n.a.	n.a.	n.a.	n.a.	n.a.	n.a.	n.a.
Colorado	-30.9	-30.9	-26.2	0.0	0.0	-6.4	-31.0	-31.0	-31.0
Florida	-17.2	-6.8	-1.7	1.4	3.7	-8.7	-16.4	-10.3	-10.3
Illinois	-19.2	-19.2	-11.9	-6.4	-6.4	-14.1	-24.4	-24.4	-24.4
Kentucky	-15.5	-15.5	-15.5	-6.7	-6.7	1.7	-21.1	-21.1	-14.1
Massachusetts	-25.8	-25.9	-25.9	-4.6	-4.6	24.2	-28.7	-29.3	-7.9
Michigan	-23.5	-24.3	-17.4	3.3	3.8	-4.9	-21.0	-21.5	-21.5
Minnesota	-31.6	-30.9	-26.8	2.6	8.2	1.9	-29.8	-25.4	-25.4
Missouri	-9.7	-9.7	-4.3	16.7	16.7	10.1	5.4	5.4	5.4
New Jersey	-17.4	-17.4	-11.9	-4.4	-4.4	-10.4	-21.1	-21.1	-21.1
New York	-16.3	-16.2	-11.9	-5.2	-5.6	-10.3	-20.5	-21.0	-21.0
North Carolina	-33.9	-34.4	-30.5	3.6	3.6	-2.2	-31.5	-32.0	-32.0
Ohio	-25.2	-25.2	-17.5	0.3	0.3	-9.0	-24.9	-24.9	-24.9
Oregon	-31.7	-31.7	-24.4	0.0	0.0	-9.7	-31.7	-31.7	-31.7
Texas	-21.5	-21.8	-16.8	0.0	0.0	-5.9	-21.4	-21.8	-21.8
Vermont	-15.4	-15.4	-15.4	0.0	0.0	4.6	-15.4	-15.4	-11.5
Virginia	-35.7	-33.7	-37.2	0.0	0.0	7.4	-35.7	-37.2	-32.6

SOURCE: Same as table 7.

n.a. Not available.

The most important factor underlying the states' failure to replace federal dollars in the case of the community services block grant apparently was their lack of financial and programmatic involvement in the community action programs before the creation of the block grant. Virtually none of the services was provided by state staff. Community Action Agencies were initially established as separate from the state governments and had operated largely independently of them. With the exceptions of Michigan and Minnesota, no state dollars were invested in the community action programs before the block grant. Unlike the community mental health centers, no mechanism existed whereby Community Action Agencies received gradually decreasing federal grants over a period of years that would require the creation of relationships with local or state sources of funding. Again, this is in contrast to the social services block grant, where the state governments were a major source of funding in all instances and had often formulated longstanding partnership arrangements with local governments to fund these services.

These factors were exacerbated by the fiscal pressure faced by most states between state fiscal years 1981 and 1984. State officials were preoccupied with finding ways of supporting their existing social and health services programs. To make commitments in areas where the state previously did not provide funds was almost out of the question.

The states did, however, make some attempt to use nonstate funds to protect the Community Action Agencies. States could require that local governments retain a match for community services block-grant sources, and most did, but state officials did not require that these governments assume responsibility for total funding of the independent Community Action Agencies. No well-developed mechanism existed, as in the State of New York's social services, for transferring responsibilities from state to local governments. There was no Community Services Act, as in Minnesota, which required that local taxes support social services in return for a shifting of control to local governments. Developments in the low-income home energy assistance block grant suggest that, at least in part, the transfer of energy block-grant funds to weatherization services was an attempt to aid Community Action Agencies. Kentucky's law implementing the community services block grant indicated that these community agencies should receive "priority" consideration for delivery of poverty-related services into local communities.

Intertitle transfer was less significant at least at the state level for the community services block grant. Although the local Community Action Agencies received funds from a variety of sources, few of these were under direct state control. In addition, the primary alternatives (funds from the Administration on Aging, Head Start, or the U.S. Department of Energy) were not, like Title IV(A) and Title XIX, open-ended entitlement programs, but were "fixed sum" federal programs that were themselves undergoing reduction. Whatever "refinancing" or intertitle transfer that occurred would thus be limited by the nature of the alternative funding sources and would have occurred in the individual Community Action Agencies rather than at the state level. No systematic data are available on the extent to which this might have taken place.

The net effect of low staff involvement, low financial involvement, and limited financing alternatives was essentially no state replacement of lost federal funds. This does not mean that the states simply passed through funding reductions to the Community Action Agencies on a pro-rata basis. Rather, the states used the community services block-grant resources available to them in accordance with their own priorities, as is discussed in detail in the next section.

The Distribution of Block-Grant Funds among Eligible Entities

The major programmatic change brought about by the block grants was the distribution of funds among grantees rather than among types of services. The states for the most part chose to allocate funds on the basis of the incidence of poverty within the state rather than or in addition to the historical basis that guided the Community Services Administration.[3] The redistribution that resulted had a noticeable impact. Between fiscal years 1981 and 1984, for example, the average share of community services block-grant allocations received by the largest recipient in each state fell from 27 percent of the state total to 19 percent of a much-reduced total. The typical reallocation was away from the big-city Community Action Agencies and toward rural ones. Detroit in 1981 received roughly 50 percent of the community services block-grant funds for Michigan, although only about 25 percent of the state's poor resided in that city. In 1983 the Detroit Community Action Agency received just under 43 percent of the total, a reduction that was part of the state policy goal of bringing Detroit's allocation to the 25 percent "poverty share" over a period of years. Other states show a similar pattern. In California the Los Angeles share was reduced from 36 to 27 percent of the total; Chicago was reduced from 67 percent to 41 percent.

---

3. This funding based on the incidence of poverty has been found in other studies as well. One study found that twenty-two of thirty-one states that had developed allocation criteria were using low-income population as at least one of the distribution criteria. See Institute for Local Self Government, *The Challenge of Block Grants: States Implement the CSBG*, Social Policy Series 4 (Berkeley, California, ILSG, May 1982).

Some service providers who formerly received large allocations were "zeroed out" of community services block-grant funds. In each case these were "ineligible entities" under the definitions established in the Omnibus Budget Reconciliation Act—either "limited-purpose agencies" or community development corporations[4] funded under previous Community Services Administration programs. The states, almost without exception, did not continue funding for these organizations after fiscal 1981. Accepting the apparent intent of the congressional earmark for "full purpose" Community Action Agencies, the states have focused community services block-grant funding on these agencies, to the virtual exclusion of other former service providers.

Although the states were quite consistent in wanting a reallocation of resources based on poverty, the means of achieving this were diverse. A few states, such as Arizona, simply converted from a 1982 formula based on historical levels of expenditure to a formula in 1983 based entirely on the incidence of state poverty. Most states developed formulas that provided funding on the basis of several factors, including the amount of the state fiscal 1981 award as well as the incidence of poverty in the state. Formulas of this kind help cushion the impact on agencies that had formerly received a large allotment from the Community Services Administration.

Texas developed a formula that placed an increasingly greater weight on poverty over time. This was accomplished by defining the funding as a function of the award of the *previous year* (not the base year amount) and the incidence of poverty. Over time this formula automatically assigned increasing weight to poverty and less to the historical level of funding that prevailed in 1981.[5]

Although these formulas typically placed large urban Community Action Agencies at a disadvantage, this was not inherently so. In Kentucky, for example, one such rural agency had been an early grantee from the Community Services Administration. This agency, along with the others in the largest city in the state, was disadvantaged by a formula based strictly on the incidence of state poverty.

The controversy this has caused has varied from state to state. Officials of Community Action Agency programs in Detroit and St. Louis, both losing

---

4. Community development corporations had been funded under Title VII of the Economic Opportunity Act and were not included in the community services block grant. They were to receive limited funding under a discretionary fund available to the secretary of the U.S. Department of Health and Human Services. See Jule Sugarman, ed., *Citizen's Guide to Changes in Human Services Programs* (Washington, D.C.: Human Services Information Center, September 1981), p. 29.

5. *CSBG State Plan* for state fiscal 1983—October 1, 1982 to September 30, 1983 (Austin, Texas: Texas Department of Economic Affairs, n.d.), pp. 29–30.

funds because of poverty-based formulas, have been quite unhappy with the results. By contrast, officials of community agencies in Portland, Oregon, apparently agreed to accept the reduction as an equitable means of providing services throughout the state. At public hearings in Michigan only seven of forty-one participants objected to the allocation formula that shifted community services block-grant dollars away from Detroit.[6]

Several factors help explain the consistent emergence of a state policy that allocates community services block-grant funds on the basis of the state-wide incidence of poverty. The most important are state officials' sense of what makes good policy and the implications of the wording of the federal legislation enacting the block grant. Public law 97-35 stipulated that services should be directed toward the alleviating of poverty of low-income persons. A number of state officials indicated that as far as they were concerned, the existing pattern of Community Services Administration funding bore no relation to poverty in their respective states. Interviews during the preparation of this book suggest that the arbitrariness (as viewed by state officials) of this Community Services Administration funding became evident only when the intrastate incidence of poverty was compared with the awards made in the past.

Other factors encouraged the development of poverty-based formulas. In a number of states it was apparent that the association of Community Action Agencies itself was interested in, or at least not opposed to, a redistribution of resources. In Oregon, for example, a governor's task force made up largely of Community Action Agency association members urged that an updated formula include the 1980 U.S. census data on the incidence of poverty for the state. In several states (Kentucky, Minnesota, and, for 1984, North Carolina), the state legislature, reflecting its own priorities as well as the concerns of other groups, stipulated that resources should be allocated on the basis of state-wide poverty. This was not an effort to undermine Community Action Agencies. In Kentucky, for example, the legislature at the same time passed a law proposed and backed by these agencies that assured them of their ability to establish program priorities.

In general, once the block grant was turned back to the states, both state legislators and officials administering the community services block grant were strongly inclined to accept poverty as a rational basis for allocating the resources, and the relative incidence of poverty within the state as the most appropriate means of operationalizing poverty measures. The effect of this policy consensus was to shift resources to rural Community Action Agencies

---

6. *Michigan FY 83 CSBG Plan* (Lansing, Michigan: n.d.), p. 42.

from a number of well-established urban ones that had been favored under the federal administration of the program.

Extending Services to Unserved Areas

The states in this study were concerned with more than shifting community services block-grant dollars among existing Community Action Agencies on the basis of poverty. Virtually all states examined (sixteen of eighteen) were explicitly concerned with creating a state-wide network of Community Action Agency services—that is, they wished to extend services to the previously unserved areas in the state. Within this very broad consensus was a variety of strategies and timetables. At one extreme was Massachusetts, where state officials hoped to extend services into uncapped areas as additional revenues became available.[7] This goal has remained an unimplemented policy objective for the state. By contrast, Texas, through various means, extended services to 92 additional counties, bringing all of the 254 Texas counties under the Community Action Agency network. This was an impressive effort in administration, given the requirement that 90 percent of the funds must go to existing service providers.

To extend services to uncapped areas, states had to work around the 90 percent earmarking requirement. Officials in Virginia claimed less than 5 percent of the community services block grant for administration in order to create one additional Community Action Agency in an unserved area. State leaders in Oregon and New York used the 5 percent discretionary money at least in part to fund Limited Purpose Agencies (those that provide less than a full range of Community Action Agency services) in areas where no community agency existed or to create new agencies in unserved areas. Several states complied with the 90 percent requirement by arranging with an existing Community Action Agency to receive additional funds, which were then subcontracted to a newly created agency in an unserved area.

The most successful strategy pursued by states such as Texas and Kentucky involved persuading existing Community Action Agencies to expand their service areas. Available community services block-grant resources were allocated to counties (rather than to Community Action Agencies) so that a certain amount of money fell outside the service areas of the existing agencies. The state administering agency would then negotiate with the existing Community Action Agencies to extend services into those areas. In Texas this was a highly formal process. Potential Community Action Agencies were

---

7. *Massachusetts State Plan for the 1983 CSBG* (Boston, Massachusetts: Massachusetts Executive Office of Communities and Development, n.d.) p. 17.

chosen on the basis of their appropriateness in covering a planning district and their previous involvement in the area. Local governments were consulted and their approval of the arrangements sought. While problems were encountered in particular instances (more than one Community Action Agency wanting to serve a particular area, urban and rural areas being unable to formulate a set of common objectives, and so on), the process in general was successful.

Despite the varying means and timetables, the policy thrust was clear. States did not accept the allocation of resources established by the categorical grant program.

Shifting Resources from Existing Eligible Entities

Little consensus existed among the states in the sample on an issue considered to be important in Congress: whether the states would continue to allocate community services block-grant resources to the existing Community Action Agencies or would turn instead to alternatives, such as city and county government or other community-based organizations. In a number of states there was an apparent agreement that the existing Community Action Agencies should continue as the providers of community-based poverty services. Kentucky legislation implementing the community services block grant recognized such agencies officially and gave them primacy as recipients of these block-grant funds. In Oregon and Minnesota the local associations of counties indicated that they were not interested in taking over the services and functions of the Community Action Agencies. In other states (North Carolina and Michigan) officials in only one or two counties expressed interest in directly providing the services—typically because their particular area was unserved.

In still other states, however, the issue of which agencies should provide services has arisen in situations marked by serious debate and disagreement. Commentators in both Texas and Illinois suggested that the existence of the 90 percent earmark served to reduce the amount of conflict that otherwise might have occurred simply because it became known that the basic policy decision had already been made in the federal law. According to this view, in the absence of such a requirement the conflict between the Community Action Agencies and the cities and counties over service roles would be a more serious one. In Missouri a number of county leaders, fifteen out of one hundred in all, inquired whether their counties could provide the services of Community Action Agencies. Half of these went so far as to make a formal application to the state. In Ohio the Association of Counties introduced legislation that would have empowered the counties to designate a Community

Action Agency. This apparently was related to disagreements with a relatively few Community Action Agencies and was not intended as a means of removing service delivery responsibilities from such agencies in general. Both New Jersey and Florida intended to dedicate a substantial portion of their community services block-grant funds to provide resources directly to local governments that would have become major providers of services in particular areas. This, of course, was possible only to a reduced extent within the 90 percent requirement, particularly when it was renewed for later years of the block grant.

Colorado was one of a few western states specifically exempted from the extension of the earmark to Community Action Agencies for the second year of the community services block grant. The state developed an explicit "poverty based" allocation to counties and tried to ensure a "base level" of funding in each county.

The issue of extending community services block-grant funds to "noneligible" entities raises the question of the impact of the 90 percent earmark on the behavior of states. An examination of the eighteen states in the sample suggests that in a third of the states the 90 percent requirement effectively constrained state behavior. Florida's state law establishing new allocations was superseded by the imposition of the 90 percent requirement for a second year, and Missouri indicated that in the absence of the 90 percent rule it would have opened a number of block-grant services to competitive bidding.

In general, however, states did not make great departures from the 90 percent earmark. Florida's law called for 70 rather than 90 percent of community services block-grant funds to go to existing service providers. Colorado, exempted along with three other states from the second year continuation of the 90 percent earmarking requirement, allocated less than 20 percent of the block to serve uncapped areas.[8]

Administrative Developments after the Block Grant

The community services block grant poses an important administrative challenge to the states. The issue is not that of administrative savings through greater efficiency, particularly at the state level. The states, to the extent that they were involved with Community Action Agencies in the past, were providing only technical assistance and minimal guidance. Under the block grant they must now assume new administrative responsibilities, and the question of savings is not appropriate. The question that arises is nonetheless important

---

8. *Proposed CSBG Funding Distribution Plan* for state fiscal 1983 (Denver, Colorado: Colorado Department of Local Affairs, n.d.), p. 3.

from the point of view of federalism: what kind of administrative effort will states put forth when they must deal with a completely new set of agencies, a network that was formerly directly controlled by the federal government? Would the state effort be the minimum necessary to meet the requirements of the block grant or would it be more extensive?

Implementation of the Block Grant

As table 20 illustrates, the states in this study were consistent in their level of administrative effort. Fifteen of eighteen states offer one or more specific examples of actions that went beyond "basic" efforts to exert administrative control over the Community Action Agencies. Three states imposed financial sanctions on agencies for failure to submit reports or for other administrative shortcomings. Nine (including several states that exerted administrative control in other ways) placed a ceiling on the amounts of administrative expenses that Community Action Agencies could claim. Seven states either tightened eligibility standards or enforced programmatic requirements that required a significant shift in agency activities. Illinois, for example, reserved 10 percent of the community services block grant to be awarded on the basis of agency performance assessed in a program review.[9]

These examples indicate a desire to actively assert responsibility over the Community Action Agencies. They demonstrate that states were aware or became aware of the management problems that had beset the Community Action Program.[10] Indeed, several state officials indicated that the Community Action Agencies needed a firmer administrative hand. They responded by providing technical assistance, seminars, on-site reviews, detailed audits, and program-focused budgets.[11]

None of the eighteen states neglected basic administrative responsibilities. All had made significant administrative changes as a result of the community services block grant. In two of the three states that did not cite examples of major administrative efforts, special circumstances were present. Colorado, under the waiver granted by Congress, allocated its resources to the counties for distribution to Community Action Agencies or other entities. It thus had

9. *Illinois Community Service Block Grant, 1983 Application Revisions* (Springfield, Illinois: Illinois Department of Commerce and Community Affairs, n.d.), p. 1.

10. *Internal Control Weaknesses Contributed to the Mismanagement and Misuse of Federal Funds at Selected Community Action Agencies*, Report AFMD-81-54 (Washington, D.C.: U.S. Government Accounting Office, July 10, 1981).

11. Kentucky, for example, set aside a specific amount for a state agency to audit community services block-grant service providers. See *Community Service Block Grant Audit Guide*, Attachment 5 (Frankfort, Kentucky: Kentucky Cabinet for Human Resources, Department of Social Services, August 1982).

TABLE 20

STATE ADMINISTRATIVE EFFORTS IN IMPLEMENTING THE COMMUNITY
SERVICES BLOCK GRANT, SELECTED STATES

State	*Selected Features of Basic Administrative Effort*	*Specific Evidence of Efforts Beyond Basic Administrative Effort*
Arizona	Proposal required for all awards Awards must reflect state priorities	Shifted focus from advocacy to service Removed weatherization services from Community Action Agencies
California	Required an accountant's prefunding certification for new grantees Required annual audit of agencies	Persuaded to defund one agency for administrative problems (in fiscal 1982, before formally accepting the block grant)
Colorado	Shifted funding and administrative responsibility to counties	
Florida	Required monthly fiscal reporting Required funding application with measurable objectives	Limited claimable administrative costs to 15 percent Lower income standards for client eligibility
Illinois	Offered technical assistance on management issues Required measurable objectives in revised application	Allocated 10 percent of dollars on basis of administrative and program performance Limited administration component
Kentucky	Developed detailed audit guide Developed specific standards for Community Action Agency administration	Limited administrative expenses to 8.5 percent of total Severely limited ability to carry forward dollars beyond one budget period

TABLE 20 (Continued)

State	Selected Features of Basic Administrative Effort	Specific Evidence of Efforts Beyond Basic Administrative Effort
Massachusetts	Offered fiscal technical assistance and training Developed detailed application package Developed detailed block-grant state regulations Implemented Performance Standards project	Defunded one agency for administrative problems
Michigan	New application procedures, including funds from all sources Oversaw financial and program, including desk and field audits for all agencies on a three-year cycle	Limited administrative costs to 25 percent of total
Minnesota	Established new comprehensive state regulations to govern programs Required annual audits by independent public accountants plus state-level audits	. . .
Missouri	Required request for proposal (RFP) process from all grantees Required unit cost for budget data Made awards on the basis of projects, not general activities	Limited administrative costs claimable Imposed state priorities (for example, parent aid program directed at child abuse) Would have contracted out a portion of dollars on competitive basis if 90 percent rule had not been in effect
New Jersey	Revised budget format Imposed requirements for direct tracking and performance reporting	Established spending ceilings for specific activities, including administration
New York	Offered fiscal technical assistance to grantees Established new application and review procedure Required yearly audits	Comprehensive audit of all federal funds received by Community Action Agencies

North Carolina	Required monthly and quarterly fiscal reports Developed, implemented state standards for local administration Offered technical assistance and training	Allowed no administrative costs; required allocation of overhead to specific services Required focusing of dollars on state service priorities
Ohio	Implemented auditing of all agencies Offered technical assistance and comprehensive training	Limited administrative costs to 10 percent of total Authorized withholding of funds for poor performance or noncompliance with contract provisions
Oregon	Required quarterly financial reports Required submission of monthly minutes of board meetings	Withheld funds for failure to provide adequate fiscal reporting Limited administrative costs to 10 percent of total
Texas	Provided training and technical assistance to Community Action Agencies Developed monitoring and evaluation schedules to assess agency performance	Reorganized weatherization program; forced Community Action Agencies to bid competitively to offer services
Vermont	Offered training in management Developed monthly financial reporting system Developed monthly report on service recipients	
Virginia	Required quarterly financial and program reporting Developed fiscal management requirements for local Community Action Agencies	Required Community Action Agencies to serve only those under the poverty line, rather than 125 percent of poverty

SOURCE: Same as table 15.

few administrative responsibilities at the state level. Minnesota, as mentioned, had for several years made substantial state contributions to the Community Action Agencies. The reporting and compliance mechanisms were already in place.

To the extent that competent, thorough administration was an issue in the community services block grant, the states appear to have passed the test. Although the federal government does not exert direct control, it would appear that the Community Action Agencies are, if anything, more closely scrutinized under the block grant than under the categorical program.

The Emergency Jobs Appropriations Bill

The Emergency Jobs Appropriations bill appropriated $25 million to the community services block grant program. The purpose of the appropriation, according to Congress, was to provide additional humanitarian assistance to the unemployed and disadvantaged. The jobs bill stipulated that to the extent possible, states should target these funds to areas in the state with the highest and most sustained rate of unemployment and to programs that would have the most immediate positive impact.

Table 21 shows that most states were able to distribute the stipulated funds in fiscal 1983, but that for the most part they did not target the monies to high-unemployment areas.

Only Arizona and Colorado distribute the jobs bill funds in a way designed to reach community service agencies or counties in areas hardest hit by unemployment. All other states simply add monies to the basic community services block-grant allocation. Colorado and New York provide an instructive contrast. Colorado distributed funds from the jobs bill to the sixteen counties in the state with the highest and most sustained unemployment rate. The stated objective was to use the funds to expand services for the unemployed. Funds were targeted to counties with unemployment rates over 15 percent or an increase of more than 5 percentage points since 1980. The state instructed service providers to focus the funds on job creation, job training, placement, and humanitarian assistance to the unemployed. In New York, however, officials decided that all entities receiving community services block-grant funds in state fiscal 1983 would also receive a portion of jobs bill funds in the form of a 6 percent supplement. State leaders decided that this allocation was both "appropriate and expedient" and the only way to fulfill the congressional intent of spending the funds quickly.

TABLE 21

EMERGENCY JOBS APPROPRIATIONS BILL AND COMMUNITY SERVICES BLOCK-GRANT FUNDS, SELECTED STATES, STATE FISCAL YEARS 1983 AND 1984

State	Funds Allocated (Millions)	Distribution Time Frame	Allocation Method
Arizona	0.286	1983, 1984	Selectively to grantees serving areas hardest hit by unemployment
Colorado	0.212	1983	To the sixteen counties with highest, most sustained unemployment
Florida	0.64	1983	Across the board to all block-grant grantees (approximately 8 percent of block grant)
Illinois	1.37	1983	Across the board to all block-grant grantees (approximately 8 percent of block-grant allocation)
Kentucky	0.456	1984	Across the board to all block-grant grantees
Michigan	1.219	1983	To all block-grant "eligible entities" (approximately 10 percent of total allocation)
Minnesota	0.300	1983	Across the board to all block-grant grantees (approximately 5 percent of block grant allocation)
Missouri	0.487	1983	Across the board (approximately 6 percent of block-grant allocation)
New Jersey	0.569	1983	Across the board (approximately 6 percent of block-grant allocation)
New York	1.621	1983	Across the board (6 percent of block-grant allocation)
North Carolina	0.500	1983	Across the board
Ohio	1.392	1983	Across the board
Oregon	0.316	1983	Across the board
Texas	0.99	1983	Across the board (4 to 5 percent of block-grant allocation)
Vermont	0.05	1984	Across the board (5 percent of block-grant allocation)
Virginia	0.366	1983, 1984	Across the board

SOURCE: Unpublished data collected by The Urban Institute from interviews with state administrators of the Emergency Jobs Appropriations bill.

CHAPTER FOUR

LOW-INCOME HOME ENERGY ASSISTANCE

The low-income home energy assistance block grant created a "block" out of only two closely related categorical programs—the Low-Income Energy Assistance program administered by the U.S. Department of Health and Human Services and the Energy Crisis Intervention program overseen by the Community Services Administration.[1] From the point of view of federalism, then, the energy block grant poses a relatively straightforward test of the question, "what will states do when they are able to design and administer a program themselves that they had run previously under a high degree of federal supervision?" Freed of many federal restrictions, states could radically change the preexisting program. Alternatively, they could leave the preblock policies and procedures virtually intact. The extent of change represents one measure of the correspondence between federal and state priorities.

The energy block grant also was unique among the block grants because it did not reduce the level of program funding (see table 22). Instead, there was a slight dollar increase in federal allocations from fiscal 1981 to fiscal 1982. Funding increased each year thereafter through fiscal 1985. States thus were free to make (or not to make) administrative changes without the pressure of spending reductions.

The energy block grant also differs from most other block grants because Congress did not write into it a series of earmarking requirements, such as the requirement in the community services block grant that 90 percent of the dollars go to fiscal 1981 service providers. Instead, the energy block grant gives the states several options to provide energy assistance in ways that had

---

1. A thorough review of the 1980 energy program is contained in *The 1980 Low Income Energy Assistance Program: A Review and Assessment* (Cambridge, Massachusetts: Urban Systems Research and Engineering, Inc., August 1981).

TABLE 22

Change in Low-Income Home Energy Assistance Expenditures, Selected States and State Fiscal Years, 1981–84

State	1981		1983		1984			Percentage Change, Low-Income Home Energy Assistance (LIHEA) Funds					Percentage Change, Total Energy Funds[c]		
	LIHEA[a]	Total[b]	LIHEA[a]	Total[b]	LIHEA[a]	Supplemental Funds	Total[b]	1981–83	1983–84	1983–84[c]	1981–84	1981–84[c]	1981–83	1983–84	1981–84
Arizona	5.7	5.7	7.2	7.2	6.7	0.8	7.5	26.3	−6.9	4.2	17.5	31.6	26.3	4.2	31.6
California	75.4	80.7	80.5	84.2	84.0	9.2	98.0	6.8	4.4	15.8	11.4	23.6	4.3	16.4	21.4
Colorado	27.7	33.5	26.7	33.3	23.3	3.2	30.2	−3.6	−12.7	−0.8	−15.9	−4.3	−6.2	−9.3	−14.9
Florida	24.3	26.4	25.0	25.6	21.6	2.7	24.9	2.9	−13.6	−2.8	−11.1	0.0	−3.0	−2.7	−5.7
Illinois	92.0	92.0	109.5	109.5	107.1	11.6	118.7	19.0	−2.2	8.4	16.4	29.0	19.0	8.4	29.0
Kentucky	23.8	29.3	29.4	29.4	24.2	2.7	30.6	23.5	−17.7	−8.5	1.7	13.0	0.3	−4.8	4.4
Massachusetts	79.8	99.5	82.7	106.5	78.5	8.4	106.6	3.6	−5.1	5.1	−1.6	8.9	7.0	−2.9	10.2
Michigan	107.8	194.0	92.7	150.7	96.0	11.0	190.2	−14.0	3.6	15.4	−11.0	−0.7	−22.3	−26.2	−2.0
Minnesota	67.8	92.7	74.3	92.0	72.1	7.9	89.8	9.6	−2.7	7.7	6.3	18.0	−0.8	−2.4	−3.1
Missouri	33.0	34.5	41.5	42.1	36.9	4.6	41.8	25.7	−11.1	0.0	11.8	22.0	−0.8	21.0	21.6
New Jersey	64.8	64.8	75.8	75.8	61.1	7.8	68.9	17.0	−19.4	−9.1	−5.7	6.3	17.0	−9.1	6.3
New York	215.7	232.2	243.4	257.2	208.4	25.4	253.3	12.8	−14.4	−3.9	−3.4	8.4	10.8	−1.5	9.1
North Carolina	32.0	32.0	34.8	34.8	37.5	3.8	41.3	8.8	7.8	18.7	17.2	29.1	8.8	18.7	29.1
Ohio	88.0	147.6	98.6	151.0	94.5	10.3	155.7	12.0	−4.2	6.3	7.4	19.1	2.3	−3.1	5.5
Oregon	20.1	22.2	24.3	26.0	20.8	2.5	25.5	20.9	−14.4	−4.1	3.5	15.9	17.1	−1.9	14.9
Texas	39.2	43.0	42.9	45.0	42.9	4.5	50.0	9.4	0.0	10.5	9.4	20.9	4.6	11.1	16.3
Vermont	10.5	13.3	12.2	14.3	11.1	1.2	13.7	16.2	−9.0	0.8	5.7	17.1	7.8	−4.2	3.2
Virginia	36.4	39.0	39.3	41.6	33.9	3.9	40.8	8.0	−13.7	−3.8	−6.9	3.8	6.7	−1.9	4.6

Source: Same as table 7.

a. Low-income home energy assistance funds for fiscal years 1983 and 1984 *exclude* funds transferred to other blocks or carried over to the next year and *include* expenditures from funds carried over from previous year and U.S. Department of Energy oil escrow funds used for energy assistance.

b. Total expenditure figures include federal low-income home energy assistance funds, state funds, and categorical programs operated by the Community Services Agency and the Department of Energy.

c. Includes supplemental funds.

not been available to them before.[2] For example, states could now reallocate up to 15 percent of the funds previously targeted for fuel assistance to payments for weatherization services. In the predecessor program under the Department of Health and Human Services, weatherization was not a permitted use. Also, the grant required that the states spend "a reasonable amount" for energy-crisis intervention services but did not further restrict the states' options. In the predecessor program a limit of 3 percent was placed on the use of low-income energy assistance funds for energy-crisis intervention to complement the energy-crisis program being administered by the Community Services Administration.

Finally, the previous energy program as a categorical grant had somewhat different goals from the programs combined into the other block grants.[3] It had not been a program of "services," that is, activities carried out by professional or volunteer staff on behalf of recipients. Rather, it consisted primarily of direct payments to or on behalf of individuals to alleviate the burden of rising costs of home energy. Most states made some direct cash payments to eligible households. These payments were more frequently made in the warmer southern states having relatively low benefits; in colder northern states the strong preference was to make payments directly to fuel vendors and utility companies on behalf of eligible recipients. Thus the previous energy program was much closer to a targeted income transfer program such as Medicaid, food stamps, or housing subsidies than to a service program.

Programmatic Developments in the Energy Block Grant

The major programmatic changes in low-income energy assistance that occurred as a result of the transition to the block grant can be directly related to the unique characteristics of the energy block grant and the predecessor program from which it was created.

Expanded Range of Activities

The most obvious change that occurred with the introduction of the block grant is that seventeen of eighteen states in the sample chose to deemphasize

---

2. Previous federal involvement in energy assistance is reviewed in Donald E. Rigby and Charles Scott, "Low-Income Energy Assistance Program," *Social Security Bulletin*, vol. 46, no. 1, January 1983, pp. 11–32.

3. See *Low Income Energy Assistance Program: Report to Congress for Fiscal Year 1981* (Washington, D.C.: U.S. Department of Health and Human Services, Social Security Administration, Office of Family Assistance, Office of Energy Assistance, August 31, 1982).

fuel assistance payments on behalf of eligible recipients in order to place
greater emphasis on immediate energy-crisis benefits, long-term weatherization benefits, or both. In the extreme case, California reduced payments
for heating and cooling costs from 93 percent of total expenditures in state
fiscal 1981 to 51 percent of total expenditures in state fiscal 1984. During
the same period Kentucky reduced its share of heating and cooling payments
from 78 percent to 25 percent. Although there are state-by-state differences,
this pervasive trend was shared by large and small states and by northern and
southern states. The data in the sample thus indicate that states used their
block-grant flexibility to expand the range of energy assistance activities (see
table 23).

Shifting of Funds to Other Block Grants

A second significant change was the trend toward state transfer of energy
dollars to other block grants. A number of state officials were quite explicit
in describing their transfers of funds out of the energy block as a "balancing"
strategy, that is, an attempt to "even out" the funding reductions in the block
grants. Because the energy program had not been cut, a number of state
officials thought that a certain portion of its resources might legitimately be
used for other purposes. The social services block grant, for example, had
taken sharp and sudden reductions. So, too, had Community Action Agency
programs. An energy block-grant transfer to the social services block grant
or the use of energy funds for weatherization (most of which was done by
Community Action Agencies) was a way to restore a portion of the funds
that had been lost in these areas.

The social services block grant was by far the most common recipient
of transfers. Ten states in the sample elected to transfer funds from the energy
block-grant program to this block grant, while two states elected to transfer
funds to the community services block grant and two to the maternal and
child health block grant. Balancing was the almost universal rationale for this
transfer. Florida, for example, in arguing the merits of this change in the face
of public criticism, pointed out that the recipients of energy payments were
also beneficiaries of the social services program, and insisted that to cut back
drastically some of the essential services would do more harm to the recipients
than the relatively small reduction in the direct energy subsidy they received.

Flexibility in Meeting Energy Needs

As pervasive as the transfer of funds out of the energy block grant was,
it was not as prevalent as the states' decision to take advantage of new

flexibility to address home energy needs with an expanded range of programs. The states in the sample, with a single exception, redesigned their energy budgets to assign more dollars for weatherization services. Five states created weatherization programs for the first time. This emphasis seems to be explained by two factors. First, state officials believed that in "cost-benefit" terms weatherization was superior to payments for fuel assistance. Despite early problems in implementing weatherization programs,[4] state energy officials argued that if they could lower the energy costs of high-use, low-income households through home weatherization, long-run costs would be significantly lower.

Second, there was either an implicit or explicit motivation to assist Community Action Agencies in dealing with their funding crisis. This latter factor is the more complex of the two. Indeed, there is evidence that external pressure as much as internal staff discussion led state officials to make this decision. Community Action Agencies or agencies closely related to them became advocates of weatherization in six states. Missouri, for example, noted that there was "overwhelming" support for weatherization from individuals testifying at the hearings around the state and responding to a question on a state-administered survey on the energy block grant asking whether an allocation to weatherization should be made. In Ohio Community Action Agencies lobbied the legislature to ensure that an allocation for weatherization services was included in the energy block grant. In the words of one spokesman, "The legislature was sympathetic to the CAPs [Community Action Agencies] on this issue." In Virginia the issue is continuing. Officials in that state originally set aside a small portion of the block grant for weatherization but were under continued pressure from weatherization advocates and Community Action Agencies to increase this share, which they did in fiscal 1984.

In seven other states Community Action Agencies were involved in regular contacts with the administering department and were the primary providers of the weatherization services. They were the clear beneficiaries of any allocation into weatherization from fuel assistance payments. In only three states was there evidence that the desire to support Community Action Agencies was not a factor. In Arizona and Texas, for example, state officials distributed weatherization funds on the basis of competitive bidding, which eliminated a number of the these agencies but substantially increased total expenditures on weatherization.

---

4. *Slow Progress and Uncertain Energy Savings in Program to Weatherize Low-Income Households*, Report EMD-80-59, (Washington, D.C.: U.S. General Accounting Office, May 15, 1980).

TABLE 23

CHANGE IN LOW-INCOME HOME ENERGY ASSISTANCE EXPENDITURES, BY TYPE OF ENERGY ASSISTANCE, SELECTED STATES AND STATE FISCAL YEARS 1981–84[a]

State	Heating and Cooling (Designated and Undesignated Payments for Fuel Assistance)				Weatherization (Services and Materials)				Energy Crisis Intervention (Payments, In-kind Benefits, and Services)			
	1981	1983	1984	Trend 1981–84	1981	1983	1984	Trend 1981–84	1981	1983	1984	Trend 1981–84
Arizona	100.0	56.9	58.2	Down	0.0	16.9	14.7	Up	0.0	26.2	26.5	Up
California	92.6	75.2	51.0	Down	6.0	16.1	18.0	Up	1.4	8.7	31.1	Up
Colorado	85.0	70.4	66.0	Down	12.6	16.1	30.7	Up	2.4	13.5	3.2	Up
Florida	93.7	80.1	77.2	Down	6.3	19.9	19.7	Up	0.0	0.0	3.1	Up
Illinois	98.1	76.0	80.8	Down	0.0	15.9	12.6	Up	1.9	8.1	6.5	Up
Kentucky	77.8	33.1	25.2	Down	19.7	12.0	26.0	Up	2.5	54.9	48.8	Up
Massachusetts	91.1	88.9	87.0	Down	8.9	11.1	13.4	Up	n.a.[b]	n.a.	n.a.	n.a.
Michigan	69.8	71.3	40.1	Down	12.0	9.2	17.2	Up	18.2	19.5	42.8	Up
Minnesota	73.6	72.3	82.2	Up	26.2	24.0	12.6	Down	0.2	3.7	5.3	Up
Missouri	100.0	87.1	85.5	Down	0.0	9.7	9.8	Up	n.a.[b]	3.2	4.7	Up

New Jersey	95.2	95.0	88.7	Down	0.0	1.6	7.4	Up	4.8	3.3	3.8	Down
New York	90.3	77.2	74.3	Down	8.4	15.2	17.6	Up	1.3	7.8	8.1	Up
North Carolina	100.0	90.2	80.2	Down	0.0	0.3	6.8	Up	0.0	9.5	13.0	Up
Ohio	91.9	63.2	58.0	Down	7.1	18.2	24.9	Up	1.0	18.6	24.9	Up
Oregon	89.9	79.5	74.0	Down	10.1	20.5	21.9	Up	n.a.[b]	n.a.	21.9	Up
Texas	90.7	82.8	77.0	Down	9.3	7.2	13.6	Up	0.0	10.0	13.6	Up
Vermont	75.0	70.5	71.0	Down	21.8	25.0	26.2	Up	3.2	4.5	26.2	Up
Virginia	93.6	91.3	82.4	Down	6.4	8.7	17.6	Up	n.a.	n.a.	n.a.	n.a.

SOURCE: Urban Institute data from state survey responses. Expenditure data for 1981 and 1983 as reported by states to The Urban Institute and the U.S. General Accounting Office; 1984 expenditure data as reported by states to U.S. Department of Health and Human Services, Social Security Administration, Office of Family Assistance, Office of Energy Assistance.

n.a.   Not available.

a.   Each state's total expenditures by type of energy assistance consists of federal block grant dollars, state dollars, and other federal dollars including U.S. Department of Energy weatherization funds. Arizona, Illinois, Missouri, New Jersey, and North Carolina did not report such funds; for these states weatherization expenditures are only from the low-income home energy assistance block grant. Administrative expenses are assigned on a proportional basis to each activity area.

b.   Emergency expenditures are combined with heating and cooling payments; the amount is less than 3 percent of the total.

Although the energy block grant required some expenditures on energy-crisis services, the block-grant legislation specified no specific percentage, only that it be "reasonable." As a result, the magnitude of the allocation ranged widely. On the other hand, Kentucky and Michigan in fiscal 1984 devoted more than 40 percent of energy block-grant resources to energy-crisis activities. Minnesota, on the other hand, allocated its resources to local providers with a small discretionary fund to be used primarily for energy-crisis purposes. Many of the same factors that applied to weatherization applied to the allocation for energy crisis. State officials indicated that crisis services were targeted to a highly identifiable energy need and that they were an implicit aid to the hard-hit Community Action Agencies, many of which provided emergency services under contract.

At least one state, California, indicated that its large allocation to energy-crisis services stemmed from a desire to assist the working poor. Under California's program, the beneficiaries of fuel assistance payments were primarily recipients of public aid, either Aid to Families with Dependent Children or Supplemental Security Income. Only in the crisis program could the state direct energy resources to those who were working and thus had higher incomes but who were nonetheless in need.

In summary, state officials noted several reasons for the reallocation of energy dollars. In several states reallocation to weatherization and energy-crisis programs had a greater effect on job creation or job maintenance than did payments for fuel assistance. It was also evident that state officials acted in the belief that weatherization offered a better long-term solution to the energy problems facing their recipients. Finally, in previous years the energy program in a few states had accumulated funds at the end of the program year to use for special programs (such as "cooling"). Most states placed a higher priority on weatherization or energy-crisis intervention than on a cooling program. Regardless of the specific motivation, the programmatic consequences of the shift to the block grant were clear. Given discretion, states drew a sizeable portion of the energy funds from fuel assistance payments and allocated those resources for short- and long-term energy assistance alternatives.

Administrative Changes

Given the relatively modest change that occurred in the transition from the Department of Health and Human Services predecessor program to the energy block grant, it might be expected that relatively modest administrative changes would result. Indeed, while virtually all states reported changes in their energy programs, many of these could best be characterized as refinements based on the experience of past years. Most of these might have been possible even if the categorical program had been continued. Developments in half of the states could be characterized in this way. In the remaining states, however, developments were directly related to the additional flexibility under the block grant. These changes are of two types: major shifts in the way in which the program was administered, and developments that could be considered innovations in programming or administration.

Shifts in Program Administration

Arizona and Texas made major shifts in the way their energy programs were administered. Arizona removed a number of Community Action Agencies from the weatherization program and invited competitive bidding for the contracts. Texas shifted the administration of the weatherization program from one department to another and in the process changed to a competitive bidding process. The new administering department also insisted that the labor component of any contract could not exceed 40 percent of the total (labor plus materials). This eliminated many Community Action Agencies that had been able to claim up to 60 percent of the program as labor expenses under the previous administration of the program. Finally, Massachusetts engaged in a major audit of all local energy providers and in summer 1982 found that at least four of these were deficient in financial and auditing procedures. It canceled contracts with these providers and opened competitive bidding for contracts in those areas.

The common theme in these state experiences is a desire for tighter state control, more effective use of funds, and a much greater willingness to use competitive bidding procedures to allocate scarce service dollars. Although these developments occurred in only a minority of the sample states, it is quite consistent with developments in other block grants, particularly the community services block grant.

Innovative Efforts

A number of states developed "innovative" approaches to program administration. The efforts may not be innovative in an ultimate sense, that is, states elsewhere may have adopted similar practices. However, the examples that follow were either directly related to or facilitated by the flexibility provided under the energy block grant.

Missouri developed an alternative method of paying utilities from the one that had existed under the categorical grant. It extended a "line of credit" to utilities based on the number of recipients actually served by that utility in the previous year. The utility could then draw down its funds as it received bills from the recipients. The state reported that this arrangement had drastically reduced the risk of utility shutoff.

Florida took the notion of "double social utility" to minimize the administrative costs of its energy program. The state limited its application period to six to eight weeks. Because this decision created a heavy one-time staff load, the administrative costs threatened to be quite high. To control costs, the department hired recipients of Aid to Families with Dependent Children (AFDC) and eliminated the need for permanent staffing. The program was able to operate with as few as one full-time person per local area as a result; the recipients of public assistance also gained what the department believed was useful experience in dealing with an actual job situation—hence, the double social utility.

Minnesota used a portion of the energy block-grant funds to develop a program of retrofitting for furnaces throughout the state. This program, in the state's studies, significantly reduced energy use in low-income households.

Texas dropped its application program for heating assistance and switched to making automatic payments for heating assistance to categorically eligible households. As a result of opposition by noncategorical household groups, Texas started an application program for crisis intervention.

Ohio improved the overall efficiency of its weatherization program by introducing a performance component into its formula for funding weatherization services. This performance factor, introduced in the 1983 state fiscal year and given heavier weight in planning for the 1984 state fiscal program year, included several factors. To obtain full performance funding, contractors could not allow the labor component to exceed a certain percentage of material costs. They were to serve at least certain proportions of elderly recipients, handicapped recipients, and rental units. Finally, they were held to installing a minimum dollar value of materials in a given period.

California switched in 1984 to having only one provider per region for both weatherization and crisis assistance. In essence the state created a "one-stop shopping center" for low-income energy assistance. Contractors are all nonprofit corporations that previously offered weatherization services. The objectives of this arrangement were to save money, make it easier on consumers, increase administrative efficiency by contracting with one agency per region, and provide better outreach for weatherization. Now everyone who applies for crisis assistance must apply for weatherization services.

Florida made a major computer system change to simplify the determination of energy assistance eligibility. Previously the state sent printouts to regional offices from the main office that handled all AFDC and food stamp recipients. The regional offices had to manually search for eligible recipients for energy assistance. Now, the main computer system does the search and send lists of energy eligibles to the regional offices. The new system saves time, reduces the delay in getting payments to recipients, and streamlines the process of eligibility determination.

Michigan had a large increase in state dollars contributed directly to energy assistance programs. The difference is that the state now pays an upfront lump sum for AFDC recipient fuel costs—a special need program for people whose heating allowance is used up before their need is filled. Previously AFDC recipients had to go through a much more laborious process of applying for low-income home energy assistance funds once their AFDC money was depleted. Many would have gotten the money anyway but there would have been more time consumed, more paperwork, and a much higher risk of utility shutoffs. These extra services were available previously but in a much more limited capacity. The state estimates that they will be able to serve 100,000 more people with the new system.

Improved State-Federal Relations

The elimination of categorical restrictions appears to have been important to these administrative changes even when there was no legal prohibition against such changes previously. This view is strengthened by a contrast between the states' perception of the social services block grant and the energy block grant. These two block grants are similar in that they "consolidated" only one or two programs that already were administered at the state level. When asked what features were particularly helpful about the social services block grant, state officials responded in terms of the relaxation of particular administrative requirements: the reporting requirements were less burdensome, they had greater flexibility in determining eligibility, and so forth.

Many state administrators of energy programs answered this question in a similar way. However, several of those discussing the energy block grant answered the question in terms of the attitude of the federal administrators. Energy officials in these states believed that one important change resulting from the block grant was a noticeable change in working relationships with federal administrators made possible by the greater flexibility in federal policy. For example, Oregon officials, pleased with the block grant, complained that the state's fiscal 1981 program elements had been imposed by federal officials, often over the strenuous objections of the state officials themselves. The officials cited the fiscal 1981 example of "Grizzly Mountain," a particularly cold region of the state for which federal administrators insisted the state develop a separate energy zone. State officials had unsuccessfully pointed out that very few people lived in the area and that an additional administrative distinction was useless and wasteful. Illinois spokespersons indicated that the state had fought with the Department of Health and Human Services over the development of its state fiscal 1981 energy program. Under the block grant, the state was able to pursue the kind of program it wanted largely without federal restraint. Those speaking for Michigan made almost an identical comment, indicating that its complex, multiagency energy program had undergone constant scrutiny by the federal government in fiscal 1981 but had not experienced this after the initiation of the block grant. Virginia officials expressed relief that "federal officials had finally realized that there were alternatives" to a given energy program, and that states could reasonably develop their own activities. Florida state leaders noted that the federal government was "easier to deal with" under the block grant.

It is difficult to gauge the significance of this change in working relations made possible by the shift in federal policy. States may have carried out essentially the same types of energy-related activity under the categorical program or the block grant. It is clear, however, that in the energy program in particular, several states had felt the heavy hand of federal administration. (No state made similar comments concerning the social services block grant.) The perception that this heavy hand was lifted was considered a major boon to state administrators—one that at least encouraged states to undertake new administrative and programmatic initiatives. Under the block grant, each state became accountable primarily to its public and legislature rather than to the federal government.

Transfers and Carryovers

Because the energy block grant escaped funding reductions and because of the block grants' flexible provisions for transfers and carryovers, it has been used as a "bank" by many states. Funds that accumulate in the energy block grant can be used to help finance many different human service programs.

Table 24 indicates the levels of carryover in each state. After falling dramatically at the end of state fiscal 1983, carryover funds available at the end of state fiscal 1984 for use in 1985 had a strong resurgence.[5] Most states attributed this growth to a combination of late-arriving supplemental funds,

---

5. See "Report on the Low Income Home Energy Assistance Program as Requested by the Senate Committee on Appropriation and the Committee on Appropriations of the House of Representatives," unpublished paper (Washington, D.C.: U.S. Department of Health and Human Services, Social Security Administration, Office of Family Assistance, Office of Energy Assistance, February 17, 1984).

TABLE 24

CARRYOVERS IN LOW-INCOME HOME ENERGY ASSISTANCE BLOCK GRANT,
SELECTED STATES, STATE FISCAL YEARS 1983–85
($ Millions)

State	*1982 Funds Carried over to 1983 Program*	*1983 Funds Carried over to 1984 Program*	*1984 Funds Carried over to 1985 Program*
Arizona	1.6	1.8	2.2
California	11.6	8.5	9.4
Colorado	0.2	1.8	6.0
Florida	1.6	0.1	3.6
Illinois	0.0	n.a.	4.5
Kentucky	5.4	0.0	0.0
Massachusetts	0.2	0.0	0.0
Michigan	0.0	0.0	0.0
Minnesota	5.5	2.9	5.5
Missouri	0.3	0.5	4.7
New Jersey	9.7	8.0	11.0
New York	17.8	0.0	21.5
North Carolina	7.4	n.a.	4.2
Ohio	4.1	6.7	7.1
Oregon	0.3	1.5	1.0
Texas	9.1	11.0	3.9
Vermont	0.0	0.0	0.0
Virginia	0.0	0.0	0.0
Total	74.8	42.8[a]	84.6

SOURCE: Unpublished data collected in The Urban Institute survey of program administrators.

a. Total excludes Illinois and North Carolina, for which data were unavailable.

which could not be spent completely before the end of the respective fiscal years, and uncertainty over future federal funding policy. In the face of this uncertainty, states found it prudent to carry forward greater sums of uncommitted funds in order to preserve program flexibility in the future.

CHAPTER 5

HEALTH SERVICES

Four of the nine block grants that were created in 1981 related to health programs. Of these block grants, three—maternal and child health, preventive health and health services, and alcoholism, drug abuse and mental health—combined a number of previously categorical health programs and were available almost immediately for state acceptance. The fourth block grant, which was for primary health care stood apart in that it "blocked" a single categorical program and was not available until a year later. All four grants faced significant federal funding cuts, though less than originally anticipated.

The Categorical Grant Programs

Like other block grants, the health services block grants replaced federal categorical grants earmarked for specific purposes and subject to direct federal control. These categorical grants supported health programs with diverse purposes: preserving the public health, providing medical care to specific populations, and developing particular kinds of medical services. Under the Reagan administration's approach to federalism, many of the program decisions made previously at the federal level were shifted to the states. As a step in this direction, the president's fiscal 1982 budget proposed combining twenty-five categorical health grants into two block grants—one for health services, the other for preventive health services. The proposal offered considerable new discretion to the states in the use and allocation of these funds. The health blocks were to be funded at 75 percent of 1981 categorical levels—in recognition both of the need for federal budget savings and of the potential for state administrative savings through consolidation. The twenty-five categorical programs that were combined into the health block grants accounted for the most important nonentitlement health-service grants and were the ones that had received the majority of federal categorical funds for health.

The Reagan administration accomplished many, though not all, of the 1982 budget objectives in health services. Congress consolidated twenty-one, not twenty-five, categorical programs into four, not two, block grants (see table 25), added certain restrictions on the use of block-grant funds, and imposed lower spending cuts. Of the four block grants, one failed to be implemented. After congressional action, the primary health care block grant was to encompass only the Community Health Centers program and retained so many of the previous requirements that it remained essentially categorical. Moreover, this grant was the only health block grant that could be rejected by the states; if states chose to decline acceptance, they could still participate in the continuing federal categorical program. Only West Virginia and the Virgin Islands have accepted the primary health care block grant thus far. Of the three successful block grants, two address traditional public health functions—maternal and child health and preventive health and health services; the third offers alcohol, drug abuse, and mental health programs. Each of these block grants is discussed in turn in the remainder of this chapter.

Maternal and Child Health

The maternal and child health (MCH) block grant consolidated an assortment of categorical grant programs that varied greatly in history, size, and form of federal assistance. The largest of these, the Maternal and Child Health Services program, was created in Title V of the original 1935 Social Security Act; funds for this program were distributed primarily by formula to the states. The grant supported general health care services for mothers and children. States could choose the specific services to be provided.

Beginning in the 1970s the states also were required to fund at least one special project in each of five types of federally mandated health services: maternal and infant care, comprehensive care for children and youth, dental care for children, infant intensive care, and family planning. Demonstration projects within these federal priority areas—mainly focused on locations deemed particularly needy—were historically funded by the federal government. In the period immediately before the health block grants, states received the money but were required to maintain the projects. This "program of projects" was generally less popular among state officials than the Maternal and Child Health Services program, for which states were required to match the federal award on a 1:1 basis. Most states overmatched, many by a large amount.

A second large grant program, Crippled Children's Services, was similar to the Maternal and Child Health Services program in two respects: states received federal funds by formula, and state funds generally exceeded the required 1:1 match. The Crippled Children's Services grant program, nationally funded at approximately half of what was allocated for the Maternal and Child Health Services program (see table 26), was to be used to locate and treat children with crippling conditions. Although federal regulations under both grant programs encouraged targeting to low-income or otherwise underserved clients, income-based eligibility requirements were left to the states.

Seven smaller programs were subsumed by the MCH block grant. One of these, the Maternal and Child Health Research and Training grant program, was created in connection with the Maternal and Child Health Services and Crippled Children's Services program; it supported investigation of issues surrounding high-risk pregnancy and child health, and the training of maternal and child health professionals. Awarded on a project basis, funds went largely to institutions of higher education, both public and private. Another program, Childhood Lead-Based Paint Poisoning prevention, was to screen potential lead poisoning victims. Grants were awarded directly from the federal government to local governments or private nonprofit agencies. There were fifty-two recipient agencies in fiscal 1981. States were rarely involved.

Other small grants also often bypassed states and were given directly to colleges and universities or to teaching hospitals. Nationwide in fiscal 1981 these included thirty-four adolescent pregnancy community programs, thirty-six genetics networks providing testing and counseling, forty-two sudden infant death syndrome (widely known as SIDS) projects doing research and counseling, and twenty-three hemophilia centers involved in testing some 6,000 patients and in providing research and education. Of the smaller grants, only funds for the disabled children of families receiving Supplemental Security Income always went to state governments. However, because states generally perceived federal authorizations to be delayed or fluctuating, most proceeded cautiously in implementing this program. By fiscal 1982 many states had never set up such a program or had only a minimal system in place. The SSI- Disabled Children program covered medical, social, developmental, and rehabilitative services to disabled children who were under seven years old or had never attended public schools.

The MCH block grant thus grouped two large categorical grant programs well-known to states—Maternal and Child Health Services and Crippled Children's Services—with seven much smaller programs often unfamiliar to state administrators.

Certain parts of the block-grant programs remained outside state control. Congress reserved 10 to 15 percent of the total for maternal and child health

TABLE 25

FEDERAL HEALTH BLOCK-GRANT STRUCTURE: PROPOSED VERSUS FINAL FORM

Block Grants Proposed by the Administration	Old Categorical Grants[a]	Block Grants Created by Congress
Health Services	1. Community health centers 2. Primary care research and development[b]	Primary Care (categorical programs 1 and 2)[b]
	3. Maternal and child health grants to states 4. Crippled children's services 5. SSI-disabled children's services 6. Hemophilia 7. Sudden infant death syndrome	Maternal and Child Health (categoricals 3–7, 19–21)
	8. Home health services 9. Emergency medical services	Preventive Health and Health Services (categoricals 8–9, 22–27)
	10. Community mental health centers 11. Alcoholism project grants and contracts 12. Alcoholism formula grants to states 13. Drug abuse project grant and contracts 14. Drug abuse formula grants to states	Alcohol, Drug Abuse, and Mental Health (categoricals 10–14)
	15. Migrant health 16. Black lung services	Unconsolidated (categoricals 15–18 remain categorical programs)

Preventive Health

17. Family planning services
18. Venereal disease control
19. Lead-based paint poisoning prevention
20. Genetic diseases
21. Adolescent health services
22. Hypertension
23. Health incentive grants Section 314(d)[c]
24. Health education and risk reduction
25. Fluoridation
26. Rodent control

Unconsolidated (categoricals 15–18 remain categorical programs)

27. Rape crisis and prevention centers[d]

Unconsolidated

SOURCES: Adapted from Randall R. Bovbjerg and Barbara A. Davis, "States Responses to Federal Health Care Block Grants: The First Year," *Milbank Memorial Fund Quarterly/Health and Society*, vol. 61 (Fall 1983), pp. 528–29; based primarily on Richard J. Price, *Health Block Grants*, Report 82-109 EPW, Congressional Research Service. Library of Congress, June 2, 1982.

a. The original administration proposal included twenty-six programs, but the immunization program was withdrawn from consolidation after the initial announcement. The number of categorical programs affected varies according to the definition of program used. The categorization for the *Catalog of Federal Domestic Assistance* of the Office of Management and Budget, for example, has twenty-eight categorical grants.

b. The R&D program was dropped in favor of a transitional planning grant to states for fiscal 1982 only, which was never funded.

c. Section 314(d) operated as a smaller block grant even before consolidation.

d. Not funded in fiscal 1981; originally created in 1980, it was outside the Public Health Service.

TABLE 26

MATERNAL AND CHILD HEALTH: RELATIVE SIZES OF PREVIOUS CATEGORICAL
GRANTS APPROPRIATIONS, FISCAL YEARS 1980 AND 1981
(Millions of Dollars)

Former Categorical Program	1980	1981
MCH Services (Parts A and B)	243.4	251.7
Crippled Children's Services	107.4	105.7
MCH Research and Training	30.8	30.0
SSI-Disabled Children	19.8	30.0
Lead-Based Paint Poisoning prevention	11.8	9.9
Genetic Diseases	11.6	13.1
Adolescent Pregnancy prevention	7.5	8.4
Hemophilia	3.0	3.3
Sudden Infant Death Syndrome	2.8	2.8
Total	438.1	454.9

SOURCES: Price, *Health Block Grants*; data on the division between Title V Maternal and Child
Health Services and Crippled Childrens' Services from private communication, DHHS
Public Health Service.

allocation to use on "projects of regional or national significance," to be
funded at the discretion of the Secretary for Health and Human Services.
Grants awarded through this set-aside mechanism pass directly from the federal agency to the recipients, without state involvement (unless a state agency
is the recipient). Most, though not all, previous recipients of genetics and
hemophilia program funds enjoyed continued funding from this reserve, as
did various research, training, and demonstration projects related to maternal
and child health. As a practical matter, the set-aside plan maintained categorical protection for these programs and limited state discretion over their
activities and funding levels.

Even considering the mitigating effect of the federal set-aside, the block
grant for maternal and child health gave states new responsibilities. First,
states could choose to continue previous federal funding patterns, shift funds
among these former categoricals, or create new programs altogether. Programs
receiving set-aside funding were protected from state-initiated "defunding,"
but all other programs subsumed by the block grant could be altered at state
discretion. Second, states concurrently gained new authority over those programs (and grantees) previously receiving funding directly from the federal
agency. For example, under the block grant, cities seeking funding for lead-
based paint poisoning prevention must now turn to the state for this support.

States also had fewer requirements imposed upon them under this block
grant. The federal block-grant legislation eliminated the five maternal and
child health project requirements, stating only that states must spend a "rea-

sonable amount'' on reducing infant mortality, preventable disease, and hand-icapping conditions, on increasing maternity care, on immunization, and on assessments of and services to low-income children. Specific demonstrations were no longer mandated. In addition, most planning and data reporting requirements were eliminated. States were required only to submit an annual grant application (covering the proposed use of funds), an annual report on the previous year's use of funds, and a biennial audit. These changes meant more latitude and significantly less federal paperwork for the states.

Congress did, however, retain a match requirement. States must match the entire MCH block grant at a 3:4 ratio, instead of the previous 1:1 match required for Title V formula grants. Because of the reduction in federal funding and the common past practice of overmatching, meeting the matching re-quirement has not proven unduly burdensome for the states included in this study.

Overall the MCH block grant gave states much greater flexibility in determining program priorities, services, and providers, and at the same time allowed states to shed the weight of previous administrative tasks. These welcome changes came with a price, however, for they were accompanied by federal funding reductions.

State Responses

Although some critics of the block grants feared major shifts in program structure,[1] in practice, states have proved cautious. Through the third year of block grants the only significant structural change has been in a few states that created "mini-blocks" delegating program decisions to local govern-ments. Thus, for this health block grant and for the other two, we examine how states have responded to the block grants within a relatively constant administrative and program structure.

Replacement of Federal Funding

Federal funding for the MCH block grant has followed an erratic pattern. After the initial block-grant reduction, funding rebounded strongly in fiscal 1983, largely because of a budget supplement delivered through the Emer-

---

1. U.S. Congress, Senate, Committee on Labor and Human Resources, *Health Services and Preventive Health Block Grants, 1981, Hearings before the Senate Committee on Labor and Human Resources.* 97th Cong., 1st sess., 1981. Also, U.S. Congress, House, Committee on the Budget, *Human Resources Programs and Block Grants, Hearings before the Task Force on Human Resources and Block Grants of the House Committee on the Budget.* 97th Cong., 1st sess., 1981.

gency Jobs Appropriations bill. Federal funding fell in fiscal 1984 only to recover again in 1985 (See table 27). For the period of comparison in this study, fiscal years 1981-84, federal appropriations declined by about 12 percent in the face of price inflation.

Most states appear to have found the resources necessary to sustain maternal and child health program spending. Eight of the eleven states in the sample for which complete fiscal 1984 data could be obtained reported growth in total maternal and child health expenditures between fiscal years 1981 and 1984. Six of the eleven states—Texas, Massachusetts, Vermont, Kentucky, Michigan, and Illinois—increased total spending on maternal and child health in real terms.

Where did the states find funds to offset the block-grant reductions? Some funding was drawn from unexpended carryovers that remained from the previous categorical grants. Like the other health programs, maternal and child health categorical grants often had been used to support multiyear projects that had funds remaining at the time of block-grant passage. These carryovers were used not only to smooth budget adjustments in the first year of the block grants but in many cases allowed states to continue to carry over unspent block-grant and categorical funds in subsequent years. Because of great uncertainty about the level of federal grant support that would be forthcoming in the future, the states took the precaution of stockpiling reserves to deal with future budget contingencies.

TABLE 27

FEDERAL MATERNAL AND CHILD HEALTH BLOCK GRANT AND PREVIOUS
CATEGORICAL FUNDING, 1980–85
(Million of Dollars)

Federal Fiscal Year	Appropriation	Percentage Change from Previous Year
1980	438.1	. . .
1981	454.9	3.8
1982	373.7	−17.8
1983	477.9[a]	27.9
1984	399.0	−16.5
1985[b]	478.0	19.8

SOURCES: Price, *Health Block Grants*; and Fiscal Years 1985 and 1986, *Budget of the United States Government: Appendix.*

a. Includes Emergency Jobs Appropriations bill funding. The average for 1983 and 1984 is $438.5 million.

b. Estimate.

Table 28 shows that carryovers accounted for roughly a third of spending from federal sources for the programs in the MCH block grant in fiscal 1982 and still accounted for a mean of almost 30 percent of federal funding in fiscal 1984. The use of these monies made it possible, in some states, for state spending from block-grant sources to hold up better than state receipt of new federal funds.

The states have continued their practice of stockpiling maternal and child health under the block grant. If anything, the level of unspent funds carried forward from fiscal 1984 to fiscal 1985 was higher, measured as a proportion of current grant receipts, than it was in earlier years (table 28). States cited the uncertainty surrounding federal funding as the principal justification for holding unexpended reserves of this size.

Most states also used their own budgets to help replace federal funds. Eight of eleven states increased spending from their own state resources for maternal and child health between fiscal years 1981 and 1984, seven by a margin large enough to increase real levels of state funding as well.

The states also had the option of making up for lost federal funds by requiring local governments to increase their contributions for joint state-local

TABLE 28

CARRYOVERS AS A PERCENTAGE OF MATERNAL AND CHILD HEALTH BLOCK-GRANT
SPENDING, SELECTED STATES AND STATE FISCAL YEARS

State	1982	1984	Carryover to 1985 as Percentage of 1984 Block Grant Receipts
Arizona	49.0	n.a.	n.a.
California	5.7	n.a.	n.a.
Colorado	40.9	32.6	31.8
Florida	32.4	n.a.	n.a.
Illinois	38.6	66.5	67.3
Kentucky	58.9	44.1	43.7
Massachusetts	32.6	16.6	11.5
Michigan	20.5	22.9	24.1
Minnesota	38.4	25.1	38.2
Missouri	42.5	42.7	50.0
New York	n.a.	11.1	3.6
Oregon	n.a.	n.a.	44.7
Texas	2.4	5.6	10.1
Virginia	n.a.	n.a.	64.5
Mean	32.9	29.7	35.4

SOURCE: Unpublished state survey data.

n.a. Not available.

maternal and child health activities. Between fiscal years 1981 and 1984 most states generated more local funding. In California, Michigan, Florida, and Texas this was an important part of the total replacement strategy. Florida, for example, systematically raised local matching requirements. States also could increase fees for service or collections from third-party insurers or government programs (for example, by obtaining full Medicaid payment for medical care also covered under Crippled Children's Services programs). Generally states left this decision to the service providers, many of whom did increase their fee structures. Illinois was one state that required greater use of sliding-scale fees for Crippled Children's Services. The states by and large indicated that they had already raised fees and tried to maximize Medicaid billings in the state-managed Maternal and Child Health and Crippled Children's Services programs even before the block grant. No state supplied data showing significantly increased collections after implementation of the block grant.

Program Priorities

One pattern appears to be dominant in states' program priorities. The states treated block-grant federal dollars much like their own state dollars. This meant that programs with a history of state funding support, whose benefits were spread throughout the state and were focused on population groups that citizens viewed as especially needy, fared best in the new budget competition. Programs that were concentrated in a few geographical areas and with an emphasis on population groups that are not viewed as especially needy were the losers.

The best example of a program that gained from the new block-grant legislation was Crippled Children's Services. The states had a large involvement in this program before the block grant. Crippled children proved to have wide public support, as became clear in public hearings and in expressions of local (county) priorities for maternal and child health spending. Crippled children also were to be found throughout a state, guaranteeing widespread distribution of funds. At the other extreme, the Lead-Based Paint Poisoning prevention program was widely viewed as a big-city program that had been formerly administered by the federal government without state involvement. Victims of the lead poisoning were more difficult to identify than crippled children. In almost all states, funding for the Lead-Based Paint Poisoning prevention program declined after the introduction of the block grant. Several states eliminated the program completely. Sudden Infant Death Syndrome programs were another example of programs with narrow target groups that were highly concentrated in big-city hospitals and subsequently lost ground when budgets were cut.

Several other programs occupied a middle ground. The Maternal and Child Health Services program had the advantage of being the largest state-operated program among the programs subsumed by the block grant. The state-to-local portion of the program enjoyed strong local support because the use of funds was relatively unrestricted. State officials in most states reported that this portion of the Maternal and Child Health Services program was strengthened under the block grant. Unfortunately, the spending data from the study conducted for this chapter are difficult to separate from two other elements of the earlier categorical grant programs—Maternal and Child Health Special Projects and Maternal and Child Health-Research and Training.[2]

State-Local Relations

The states confronted several issues affecting the role of local governments as they planned for implementation of the maternal and child health block grant: (1) competition between the programs traditionally was limited to certain localities—for example, the Lead-Based Paint Poisoning prevention program—in urban areas and the programs with broader or even state-wide coverage; (2) localities that previously did not receive federal funding pressed hard for greater geographic equity in the distribution of block-grant dollars; and (3) in some states the block grant encompassed both services offered at the state level and those provided locally, generating a state-local competition for funds. In most states, officials relied on the established pattern of state-local relations to deal with the block grant, but in eight of the states in the sample these issues resulted in a changed distribution of maternal and child health dollars and gave counties a larger role in their disposition.

Three states decentralized funding distributions to help areas that had received fewer funds in the past, usually nonmetropolitan counties, but kept the programs categorical. Five states went still further by creating mini-blocks with at least some portion of the block-grant funds. Of these, three chose to redistribute maternal and child health dollars so that all counties now receive a base level of funding. These mini-blocks typically gave local governments even more autonomy with new block-grant funds than they had previously with state funds. The five states that developed mini-blocks are Oregon, Missouri, Illinois, Ohio, and New York.

---

2. These elements received far less support from the states. The special projects program had had a strong big-city orientation when it was operated as a federal program. The research and training program, like other research and training programs, found it difficult to compete with direct service delivery for scarce state funding.

This new local autonomy, though in a minority of the states in the study, suggests an increasing local role in the MCH block grant that is consistent with states' preference for statewide, basic health services. Should such local autonomy become more widespread, maternal and child health services will become available to some degree in even the least populated counties, but with fewer specialized programs. In most states, this will mean a modest shift in funding distribution from urban to less densely populated areas. In addition, local governments will gain greater control over the selection of services and providers, as the increased state flexibility offered by the block grants is passed on to the local governments.

Administrative Changes

The MCH block grant offers states certain, albeit limited opportunities to streamline program administration. Elimination of lengthy planning and reporting requirements has enabled at least one of the sample states (Arizona) to reduce or reassign staff, but for the majority of states the change has simply reduced the "level of aggravation." Several states, most notably Michigan, New York, and Massachusetts, noted that state planning needs have remained constant (if not escalated in the latter state), and that needs assessments, program evaluation, and general data collection for block-grant decision making require a level of effort at least equal to that under federal requirements before the block grant. Thus it is difficult to reach any generalization regarding the administrative and fiscal effects of federal deregulation.

The consolidation of categorical programs itself offered opportunities for improved administrative efficiency in some states. Ohio, for example, plans to merge the maternal and child health programs into two basic grant programs, one for child and family health services and one for perinatal and infant care, and reorganize the Division of Maternal and Child Health Services to mirror the simpler and presumably more efficient grant structure. States like Oregon and Missouri, where mini-blocks have been created, note greater efficiency in state administration and suggest significant savings at the local level resulting from the grant consolidation and streamlined application procedures inherent to mini-blocks. Eight states integrated the SSI-Disabled Children and Crippled Children's Services programs, both for ease of reallocation and for improved efficiency. The SSI-Disabled Children program serves an income-tested subgroup of recipients of Crippled Children's Services and provides ancillary services that complement the treatment provided by the latter program. Although state officials felt this consolidation streamlined administration, they could not provide estimates of savings. Furthermore, the merging was typically accompanied by a programmatic change that eliminated many of the distinct services previously available under the SSI-Disabled Children program.

Savings resulting from deregulation and consolidation were thus often difficult to document in the MCH block grant.[3] Because it grouped programs largely already administered by a single division of the state health department, most states found little opportunity for administrative consolidation. Any savings from this block grant appeared primarily from reduced federal reporting requirements, and even these proved uneven across states and were difficult to estimate.

Preventive Health and Health Services

One small block-grant program, six former categorical grant programs, and one new program were merged to create the Preventive Health and Health Services (PHHS) block grant. The former grant programs fall into four groups.

1. One former block grant to states called the Health Incentive Grant program, or more commonly, the section "314(d)" program, distributed formula funds for "comprehensive public health services" to all states. States could use the grant for nearly anything related to state and local public health services. They commonly allocated these funds for health services administered through local health departments or for state laboratory services in support of local health departments. Historically, the 314(d) program was the largest program included in PHHS and was very popular both with states and their local government grantees. The Carter administration, however, greatly cut 1981 funds and sought to end the grant for 1982.

2. Former federal-to-state categorical grants included the Health Education Risk Reduction program, a smoking, obesity, and substance abuse prevention program for children and adolescents offered primarily in secondary schools. Most funds for this program were channeled through state health agencies to hundreds of local projects. A hypertension program supported screening, diagnostic, and referral services. Before 1980 the funds went by formula to states. In 1980 and 1981 states had to compete for funds on a project basis. Most hypertension projects called for locally provided but state-coordinated services. Fluoridation program grants often went to states for assisting localities to install new community fluoridation plants (some went

---

3. Several states did report changes in the state-run services for handicapped children (Crippled Children's Services and SSI-Disabled Children programs). Three states (Texas, North Carolina, and Illinois) have restricted eligibility for the former program through such actions as reducing the age limit for treatment.

directly to localities). Some 261 were funded in fiscal 1981. These programs existed in most states before block-grant consolidation.

3. Grants that previously bypassed the state level included those for the Rodent Control program (more often called rat control). These grants usually passed from the federal level directly to cities; sixty-eight awards were made in fiscal 1981. Grants for the Emergency Medical Services program generally funded regional coordinating entities with grants passed through the state. Funds covered planning, initial operations, and upgrading of services. The Home Health grant program supplied start-up and expansion grants to approved home health agencies.

4. One new program, the Rape Crisis Centers, was previously enacted but never categorically funded. It received earmarked funding for the first time in fiscal 1982 as part of the block grant. Funds are to pay for services to rape victims as well as for rape prevention; officials often refer to the program as rape prevention.

At first glance these disparate, mainly narrowly targeted programs appear to have been rather evenly matched for the state-level competition over funding after the block grant was introduced. No one program had been fiscally dominant before the block grant. Furthermore, local programs were not dwarfed by huge state categorical grant programs, as was the case in the MCH block grant. Table 29 shows federal appropriations for each for fiscal years 1980 and 1981. Although the Health Incentive Grant program—314(d)—was historically the biggest, it suffered the most in reductions before the block grant.

TABLE 29

PREVENTIVE HEALTH AND HEALTH SERVICES: RELATIVE SIZES OF PREVIOUS
CATEGORICAL GRANT APPROPRIATIONS, FISCAL YEARS 1980 AND 1981
(Millions of Dollars)

Former Categorical Program[a]	1980	1981[b]
Health Incentive Grant, Section 314(d)	68.0	9.0
Emergency Medical Services	32.1	30.0
Health Education and Risk Reduction	23.5	16.2
Hypertension	20.0	20.0
Urban Rodent Control	14.5	13.0
Fluoridation	6.8	5.0
Home Health	5.0	0.0
Total	169.9	93.2

SOURCE: Price, *Health Block Grants*.

a. The Rape Prevention program did not exist in fiscal 1980; in 1981 it was approved but not funded.

b. After mid-year recisions.

Fully half of the base-year PHHS block-grant expenditures (fiscal 1981) were for direct, federal-to-local programs.

Three of the eight programs merged to form the block grant were to some extent protected, at least initially, by federal earmarking and other requirements—the Hypertension, Emergency Medical Services, and Rape Prevention programs. State block-grant support for the Hypertension program could not drop below 75 percent of the fiscal 1981 grant amount in fiscal 1982, 70 percent in fiscal 1983, and 60 percent in fiscal 1984. States were required to give some funding to all fiscal 1981 local grantees of the Emergency Medical Services program in fiscal 1982 and were initially prohibited from using block-grant funds to purchase program equipment, a restriction later modified. To protect the Rape Prevention program, Congress effectively retained its categorical status, reserving a minimum allocation in each state.

On closer examination, however, the 314(d) program can be seen to have had clear advantages over the others. Because it was a former block grant itself, states had already developed general priorities for state and local uses of funds as well as a process for allocating the funds among competing public health needs. The 314(d) program had existed since 1966 and was well established. Although the fiscal 1981 recision reduced its fiscal importance that year, the program remained dominant in administrators' thinking. Indeed, the cut seems to have benefited the old 314(d) programs in the PHHS block-grant era, since 314(d) was seen as particularly "needy," having just lost funds the previous year.

Federal Cuts, State Replacement

For a time after implementation it seemed that the PHHS block grant would suffer the deepest cuts of any of the health block grants (see table 30). But its constituent programs have yet to face significant reductions in most of the sample states. The PHHS block-grant appropriations, after supplements, did not decline as steeply as foreseen. The states found that they had even larger categorical carryovers than were observed in the MCH block grant. Carryover categorical funds supported almost two-thirds of PHHS block-grant spending in the sample of states in fiscal 1982—or nearly seven and one-half months' spending at rates existing before the block grant. Large carryovers persisted into fiscal years 1984 and 1985 (see table 31). As a result, states' adjustments have been cushioned. State officials explained the large carryovers as a precaution against uncertainty regarding future federal grant policy. The block-grant reserves made it possible to continue state programs for a time, even if federal funding were cut more drastically, as several states believed was likely to happen.

TABLE 30

FEDERAL PREVENTIVE HEALTH AND HEALTH SERVICES BLOCK-GRANT
APPROPRIATIONS, FISCAL YEARS 1980–85
(Millions of Dollars)

Year	PHHS Appropriations	Percentage Change from Previous Year
1980	169.9	
1981	93.2	−45.1
1982	81.6	−12.4
1983	86.3	5.8
1984	88.2	2.2
1985[a]	89.5	1.5

SOURCES: Price, *Health Block Grants*; and *Budget of the United States Government: Appendix*, Fiscal Years 1984, 1985, and 1986.

a. Estimate.

Despite the relatively modest federal funding reductions, the PHHS block grant displays a much more mixed pattern of subsequent total spending than the other block grants. Total program spending between fiscal years 1981 and 1984 (or fiscal 1983 when that is the latest data available) declined in almost as many states (seven) as it rose (eight). State support from own resources was similarly inconsistent. Although state funding increased in nine of the fifteen states, three states eliminated state funding for the PHHS block grant completely.

Program Priorities

Almost all of the survey states have adjusted their PHHS program mix. To a very small degree, this has involved completely new programs or initiatives within programs. New York State developed a new cancer registration project, but it was the only entirely new activity we could identify. The PHHS block grant seems more amenable to structural changes than the MCH block grant, perhaps because even fewer of the previous categorical grants were state administered. Almost all of the allocative changes, however, have involved funding shifts among the old federal program categories.

State interviewees showed more agreement on what programs they intended to reduce than on those to be protected from funding cuts. Rodent Control, Home Health, Emergency Medical Services, and Health Education programs were most frequently mentioned as candidates for cutbacks. Indeed, the Rodent Control program lost funds in every state that had such a program. It was perceived as a large-city program, just as the Lead-Based Paint Poi-

TABLE 31

CARRYOVERS AS A PERCENTAGE OF BLOCK-GRANT SPENDING, SELECTED STATES
AND FISCAL YEARS, 1982, 1984, AND 1985

State	1982	1984	Carryover to 1985 as Percentage of 1984 Appropriations
Arizona	77.8	17.3	11.7
California	30.5	8.5	10.8
Colorado	75.0	49.5	0.0
Florida	73.1	n.a.	n.a.
Illinois	53.3	70.5	75.7
Kentucky	52.9	43.1	43.8
Massachusetts	68.8	58.9	56.6
Michigan	63.8	14.8	4.7
Minnesota	73.3	43.5	70.0
Mississippi	92.9	n.a.	n.a.
New York	n.a.	33.7	28.1
Oregon	n.a.	n.a.	48.2
Texas	47.5	28.7	21.7
Vermont	66.7	n.a.	n.a.
Virginia	n.a.	n.a.	100.0

SOURCE: Unpublished state survey data.

n.a. Not available.

soning prevention program was under the MCH block grant. Spending for the Home Health program also declined in all but one state.

Programs funded under the old 314(d) grant program (mostly local health), and the Hypertension and Fluoridation programs were the most favored by the sample states, though even here the record is mixed. Some states went so far as to eliminate the Health Incentive Grant structure completely.

Enlarging the Role of Local Government

A large number of states gave counties greater responsibility for PHHS services and distributed funds for these programs more evenly across the state. Seven of the eighteen states altered the pre-block geographic distribution of funds; of these, five awarded greater local discretion through "mini-blocks," a mechanism described in the discussion on the MCH block grant above. In each case, this wider distribution of funds meant an advantage for the more rural areas and a disadvantage for cities. Appendix A to this chapter describes these states' initiatives.

The shift in distribution that enabled greater county discretion also was a disadvantage for previous recipients of program funds—cities and private nonprofit agencies. For example, an urban county may choose to fund a city's Rodent Control program with its PHHS mini-block, especially if the mini-block award reflects continued funding for that program. However, if PHHS funds are at the same time shifting away from urban areas, the county may, not unreasonably, protect county-run programs (such as local health department services) from funding cuts at the expense of noncounty programs, like Rodent Control.

Though fewer than half the sample states chose mini-blocking or redistribution initiatives, their decisions probably point to a trend, since the states acted relatively quickly and despite congressional restrictions. We thus expect that these early shifts herald greater changes as this block grant matures, especially if the earmarks lapse. If so, the counties will inherit more responsibility for PHHS programs included in the block grant than for those in the other health block grants.

Administrative Changes

Some states found initial PHHS implementation time-consuming and expensive, but most agreed that the block grant eventually lightened their paperwork. In the first year of the PHHS block grant the states received administrative responsibility for programs that had previously been outside state operations. In addition, certain states, like Michigan and California, had previously administered the PHHS categorical programs in different state departments, or in several different divisions within a single department. Absorbing new programs and consolidating administration complicated implementation of the block grant and temporarily raised administrative burdens. By the second year, states had begun to appreciate the reduced federal requirements and had even begun to introduce their own further initiatives to streamline administration.

At least nine of the eighteen states (Colorado, Illinois, Minnesota, Missouri, North Carolina, Ohio, Oregon, Texas, Virginia) altered state administrative practices in response to the PHHS block grant, with a majority passing on the burden of funding reductions to local grantees. The five states with the mini-block mechanism (see Appendix A) consolidated certain state administrative procedures and requirements applicable to all local grantees. For example, these states no longer review separate applications for each former categorical, nor do they collect program-related data: funds are now distributed by formula and thus require no state-level planning process. Three other states consolidated administrative processes without the mini-block mechanism.

Minnesota, Colorado, and Virginia all adopted some form of paperwork consolidation, such as a single contract or application for all PHHS programs, thus saving some time for both state administrators and local grantees.

The fiscal impact of this reduced paperwork is not yet clear. Nearly all state officials we interviewed believed that the PHHS block grant permits greater efficiency in state administration, but virtually none claimed net budgetary savings from these administrative changes, even after the initial "planning" year. (Several state administrators stated that the savings occurred "at the local level," but had no evidence.) In most sample states administrative consolidation seems thus far to have saved staff time, generated higher quality work, or allowed individuals to focus on important but previously neglected issues. These are recognized improvements, but not significant dollar savings.

State Changes in Service Delivery

State officials could tell us even less about specific changes in services under the PHHS block grant than under the MCH block grant. States seldom provide PHHS services themselves; furthermore, especially in states that created mini-blocks, most state reporting requirements for local grantees have been reduced or eliminated. The frequent move to spread PHHS funds throughout each state, however, clearly will affect local services. On the one hand, it can be argued that devolution will broaden service availability and increase coverage statewide. On the other, this redistribution of a relatively fixed amount of money seems to require states to give up targeting funds to those most in need and may result in spreading the money so thin that little can be accomplished. The debate about redistribution has much in common with the debate about block-grant versus categorical grant targeting, and it remains too early to draw conclusions in the state and local context.

Missouri's experience is suggestive, nonetheless. That state redistributed Hypertension funding to achieve statewide coverage and found that the result was a downgrading of services and a mismatch of facilities to need. Under the previous categorical grant system, the state had awarded a few Hypertension program grants for screening, monitoring, and follow-up services to areas with the greatest medical need. Beginning in state fiscal 1982, Missouri spread Hypertension program resources to all counties, but limited eligible services to hypertension screening. After almost two years with this new system, state health officials concluded that Missouri's highest incidences of hypertension are indeed in the areas funded before state fiscal 1982, is minimal elsewhere, and that these Hypertension program funds could be more productively spent under a system that provided not only screening but also additional services in proven high-incidence areas.

Among the sample states Missouri offers the sole example of a reversion to targeting; its decision to target funds was made only for the Hypertension program, a program planned for a mini-block in only one other state. That Missouri decided to reinstitute narrow targeting after its initial enthusiasm for spreading funds statewide does show, however, that one can expect more shifts as the states continue to decide how best to spend PHHS block-grant funds.

Alcohol, Drug Abuse, and Mental Health

In consolidating federal alcohol, drug abuse, and mental health categorical programs, Congress placed more restrictions on states' use of block-grant funds than in either of the two other health block grants. These restrictions limited state reallocations of funds, protected certain pre-block grantees, and constrained state decisions regarding services provided. On the other hand, the block grant allowed states to consolidate loosely coordinated parallel programs into a single, integrated, federal-state-local system of funding and service provision. Because the alcohol, drug abuse, and mental health programs in states and localities already paralleled the federal categorical grant programs, the consolidation had considerable potential for administrative and delivery efficiencies.

As is true of the other block grants, understanding the alcohol, drug abuse, and mental health (ADM) block grant requires a knowledge of its categorical antecedents. Table 32 shows the three main types of categorical grants subsumed by this block grant and their funding levels (see also table 33).

The first type of program grants was the Community Mental Health program. Begun in 1963 to help build centers to provide noninstitutional care, this program grew to provide categorical support for independent, nonprofit Community Mental Health Centers, widely referred to as CMHCs. Of the major CMHC categorical grants, initial operations, the largest and most common grant, subsidized new CMHCs for eight years, with annually declining grants intended to ease the transition for recipients of federal dependence; other grants supported consultation and education services in CMHCs. Financial distress awards helped support some CMHCs up to five years beyond their initial eight, and staffing grants provided continuation support (no new grants in fiscal years 1980 or 1981) for staff for new services. All funds passed directly from the federal government to the recipient CMHCs. Except where states themselves were CMHC grantees, there was little state involvement. However, states did help review and monitor the small construction

TABLE 32

ALCOHOL, DRUG ABUSE, AND MENTAL HEALTH: RELATIVE SIZES OF PREVIOUS
CATEGORICAL GRANT APPROPRIATIONS, FISCAL YEARS 1980 AND 1981
($ Millions)

Program and Component	1980	1981
Community Mental Health	293.5	277.6
Initial operations		
Consultation and education		
Financial distress		
Staffing		
Other miscellaneous		
Alcoholism	116.0	71.5
Formula grant		
Projects mandated by Uniform Treatment Act[a]		
Other projects		
Drug Abuse	196.5	170.3
Formula grant projects		
Treatment demonstration projects		
Statewide services		
Total ADM appropriations	606.0	519.3

SOURCE: Price, *Health Block Grants.*

a. Special grants were made to promote state adoption and compliance with the model Uniform Alcoholism and Intoxication and Treatment Act under Section 310 of the Comprehensive Alcoholism, Drug Abuse, and Mental Health Act of 1970, as amended; this authority was repealed by the Omnibus Budget Reconciliation Act of 1981.

portions of the federal grants, and many CMHCs also dealt with states in receiving some state mental health funds as well as Medicaid payments.

The second type of program grant was the Alcoholism program. Until the federal 1981 aid recisions, the state formula grant was seen as the most important of five alcoholism grants. It funded all states, by formula, for alcoholism prevention, treatment, or rehabilitation programs. States had general allocative discretion so long as their efforts fell within these broad categories. The only major restriction was that annual administrative costs could not exceed 10 percent or $50,000, whichever was the lesser amount.

States also received a small amount of special project funds to support the federal goals of enacting a state model law to govern alcoholism services. Three other, larger project grants made federal awards directly to service providers—states, local governments, or private nonprofit agencies. States thus controlled less than half of the federal alcoholism dollars—and far less than that after the drastic federal recision of the formula funds in fiscal 1981. Direct federal grants allocated most of the pre-block funds.

TABLE 33

FEDERAL ALCOHOL, DRUG ABUSE, AND MENTAL HEALTH BLOCK-GRANT
APPROPRIATIONS, FISCAL YEARS 1980–85
(Millions of Dollars)

Year	ADM Appropriations	Percentage Change from Previous Year
1980	625.1	
1981	585.3	−6.4
1982	432.0	−26.2
1983[a]	469.0	8.6
1984	462.0	−1.5
1985[b]	490.0	6.1

SOURCES: *States Have Made Few Changes in Implementing the Alcohol, Drug Abuse, and Mental Health Services Block Grant*, U.S. General Accounting Office, June 1984; and *Budget of the United States Government: Appendix*, Fiscal 1986.

a. Includes Jobs bill funding.
b. Estimate.

Federal grants for Drug Abuse, the third type of categorical program grant, also included both formula and project awards, but there the resemblance to alcoholism grants ends. States saw the medium-sized drug abuse formula grant to states as much more restrictive than its counterpart for alcoholism. It was geared to prevention programs and funded far fewer direct treatment services than did alcoholism grants. The federal aid recisions of fiscal 1981 also cut these formula grant funds.

Conversely, the drug project grants offered states more control than they had over alcoholism projects. Whereas most alcoholism grants were awarded directly to the service providers, only one small grant program for drug treatment demonstration projects was administered that way. The statewide services treatment grants, providing nearly three-quarters of the federal drug abuse aid, were awarded to states on a project, not formula, basis. The federal agency determined which particular state proposals (often more than one per state) would receive funding; the states ran the projects and chose the ultimate service providers themselves.

Block-Grant Restrictions and Opportunities

The ADM block grant set up a two-tiered funding split among the three categorical grant functions described above. First, states had to spend at least a minimum share of the block grant on "substance abuse"; then, they had to allocate minimum shares of substance-abuse funds to both alcoholism and drug abuse. The grants imposed other restrictions as well. Appendix B to this chapter summarizes the major restrictions.

Despite these allocative earmarkings, states gained new control over federal funds and service providers. These newly available funds included all CMHC grants, a substantial portion of alcoholism project grants, and a comparatively small number of drug abuse grants. States could reallocate most funds to different functions within each program area and could largely fund the service providers of their choice.

Moreover, states could improve the efficiency of the funding system by consolidating formerly separate federal and state programs to a greater degree than they could for either of the other two health block grants. The federal ADM programs previously supplemented or paralleled grant systems in nearly all eighteen states. All these states preside over community mental health budgets that dwarf the federal CMHC program, and all but one have also made state financial commitments to both alcohol and drug abuse programs.

By eliminating the federal alcohol and drug reporting requirements, the block grant expanded the potential for administrative savings even further. Previous service-provider grantees were required to report extensive service and recipient-related information. State data requirements appear to be less burdensome. Grantees formerly required to report to both federal and state government (on two different forms) would gain the most from reduced requirements.

Overall, the ADM block grant offered an opportunity not found in the other health block grants to increase efficiency and eliminate federal-state programmatic duplication, despite the nearly categorical restrictions of the ADM on reallocations among program areas.

Federal Cuts, State Replacement

The ADM block-grant appropriations dropped sharply between 1980 and 1982. Federal recisions in 1981 had selectively reduced the aggregate categorical funding, and block-grant appropriations further reduced support for alcohol, drug abuse, and mental health programs by 26.2 percent the following year (see table 33).

However, carryover funds cushioned the ADM block-grant adjustments, just as it did for the MCH and PHHS block grants. On average, for the states in the sample reporting usable data 71 percent of fiscal 1982 spending from federal funds for the ADM block grant came from carryovers—enough to cover about eight and one-half months of fiscal 1981-level spending. Unexpended reserves have been drawn down more rapidly for the ADM block grant than they have for the other two health block grants, but remained sufficient in fiscal 1984.

States spent carryover funds first (or had their service-provider grantees do so), then drew from block-grant funds, often in turn carrying forward block-grant funds for future use. This cushion helped smooth the fiscal effects of abrupt appropriation changes and "bought" time needed to achieve an orderly transition from the old categorical system to block grants. A few states were even able to support some activities with federal funds at levels prevailing before the block grant was introduced through fiscal 1984, fully three years after the funding cuts associated with block-grant consolidation.

To what extent alcohol, drug abuse, and mental health service providers were affected by block-grant related cuts also depended on what happened to state and local support. Overall, state and local replacement was very good. Sixteen states managed to increase total ADM service program spending in the face of federal aid reductions. Fourteen of sixteen states increased their own state budgets for such services and nine of these states raised them at a rate greater than general price increases, with the result that real state funding from own sources rose as well (see table 34).

Changing the Program Mix

Program reallocations were rather limited across the three program areas within the ADM block grant. Typically, states preferred to maintain historical funding shares of federal funds at least in the first year of the block grant, state fiscal 1982. They relied on carryover funds to fill the funding gaps until planning for fiscal adjustments could be completed. However, four states were prevented from maintaining the status quo by the two-tier federal allocation formula (described in appendix B to this chapter). For them, ironically, the impetus for a new method at reallocating came not from the lifting of past categorical requirements, but rather from the newly imposed block-grant earmarks.

New York, California, New Jersey, and Virginia discovered that their alcoholism programs received less than the required 35 percent of federal substance abuse dollars in 1981. A pro-rata division of the block-grant funds between alcoholism and drug abuse—the distribution method most states preferred—would thus have violated the federal "35 percent" requirement (see table 34). As a result, these states had to shift federal funds for services from drug abuse to alcoholism.

By state fiscal 1983 the funding situation had worsened in nearly all eighteen states, necessitating some fiscal adjustments. In contrast to the experience in the MCH and PHHS blocks grants, however, states have only rarely strayed from the historic federal funding shares (except to comply with federal rules). With regard to block-grant funding, much of the reason for this apparent continuity may lie in the federal earmarkings. Under the block-grant rules, only 5 percent of fiscal 1983 federal funds were not earmarked to be spent according to the historical shares of mental health and substance abuse; within these two areas, further earmarks dictated which mental health service-provider grantees to fund and how to divide funds between services for alcoholism and drug abuse. States did not have much reallocative flexibility, even if they wanted to use it.

Nonetheless, most states did not exercise the little flexibility available. Nearly all eighteen states also split the ''free'' 5 percent of the block-grant pro rata. Those not choosing this approach awarded the discretionary amount to whichever program seemed most disadvantaged by the block grant. For example, New York used the 5 percent to compensate the drug program for the federally mandated shift of funds to alcoholism. There was equally little interest in departing from past patterns in allocating the 30 percent of substance abuse allowed to be spent however the state wanted. State officials apparently liked the allocation before the block grant and maintained it. Indeed, interviewees in nearly all our eighteen states spoke of maintaining historical funding shares for all funds as well as for block grants. States' apparent lack of reallocative zeal here, compared with the other health block grants, may reflect the three ADM program areas' more nearly equal sizes and degree of past state involvement and support. The ADM block grant includes no small, completely federal categorical programs. This block grant presented no such obvious targets for cuts as the special federally funded MCH projects or Rodent Control programs. Rather, states were already heavily involved in ADM functions and hence were little inclined to make rapid changes in past funding patterns.

A different, and clearer, pattern of reallocation is developing *within* the alcoholism and drug abuse programs. It results from the new federal earmarking for prevention. In contrast to the other health block grants in which states favored direct treatment over prevention and other indirect services, the few states making reallocations within substance abuse shifted support *to* prevention *from* treatment. These shifts point to the prevention requirement of the ADM block grant. The requirement specified that at least 20 percent of substance abuse spending be used to support prevention, a higher percentage than some states had historically spent from both federal and state funds together. Most states, however, were either already spending 20 percent of categorical federal funds on prevention or could easily adjust to spend 20 percent of block-grant funds on large, existing state prevention programs while shifting some formerly federal treatment services to state support. A

TABLE 34

CHANGING FUNDING SOURCES FOR ALCOHOL, DRUG ABUSE, AND MENTAL HEALTH SPENDING, SELECTED STATES, STATE FISCAL YEARS 1981–84
(Millions of Dollars)

State and item	1981	1984	Percent Change 1981–84
Arizona			
Block grant and carryover	9.9	12.9	30.2
State	16.8	17.1	1.6
Total[a]	36.6	45.1	23.4
California			
Block grant and carryover	54.3	43.5	-19.9
State	397.9	426.0	7.1
Total	531.7	585.6	10.1
Colorado			
Block grant and carryover	9.2	7.6	-17.8
State	26.8	26.2	-2.4
Total	52.2	54.3	4.0
Florida			
Block grant and carryover	32.0	30.8	-3.9
State	35.5	62.6	76.4
Total	90.0	104.5	15.0
New Jersey			
Block grant and carryover	2.6	23.4	-9.7
State	26.4	16.9	-36.0
Total	56.3	41.0	-27.2
New York			
Block grant and carryover	51.6	n.a.	n.a.
State	144.4	n.a.	n.a.
Total	384.0	n.a.	n.a.
North Carolina			
Block grant and carryover	12.3	9.9	-19.7
State	33.3	49.4	48.2
Total	76.2	101.5	33.2
Oregon			
Block grant and carryover	4.5	n.a.	n.a.
State	7.1	n.a.	n.a.
Total	11.6	n.a.	n.a.

Kentucky			
Block grant and carryover	5.2	3.4ᵃ	−34.6ᵃ
State	6.1	9.9ᵃ	62.3
Total	31.8	29.3ᵃ	−7.9
Massachusetts			
Block grant and carryover	23.2	18.5ᵃ	−20.6
State	46.7	61.9ᵃ	24.6
Total	73.4	82.8	12.8
Michigan			
Block grant and carryover	11.8	11.2	−5.1
State	19.0	21.4	12.6
Total	50.7	60.6	19.5
Missouri			
Block grant and carryover	11.2	7.2	−35.7
State	6.6	1.8	78.8
Total	21.0	20.8	−0.8
Pennsylvania			
Block grant and carryover	30.5	26.7	−12.7
State	110.3	124.5	12.9
Total	170.1	188.6	10.9
Texas			
Block grant and carryover	21.7	23.9	9.8
State	25.0	52.1	108.0
Total	61.0	98.9	62.1
Vermont			
Block grant and carryover	4.8	3.5	−27.1
State	3.7	7.9	113.5
Total	15.7	18.8	19.7
Virginia			
Block grant and carryover	8.5	7.2	−15.4
State	6.5	11.4	75.1
Total	23.0	20.5	−10.7

SOURCE: Data provided by states. Figures are rounded.

a. State fiscal year 1983.

few states found the definition of "prevention" sufficiently flexible to enable them to continue existing funding patterns, despite their apparent inconsistency with federal allocation requirements.

Actual shifts in total spending were prompted by the federal rules, however. In Texas federal recisions in the drug prevention formula grant left practically no federally funded prevention programs as the block grant took effect, and no General Fund dollars were previously spent on this function. In state fiscal 1984, when carryover funds were no longer available, Texas shifted funding from drug treatment to prevention in order to meet federal requirements. Other states have faced (or will face) less drastic difficulties, but at least five must somehow alter their mix of programs—in all cases either moving federal funds from treatment to prevention or "finding" new state dollars to support such a shift in federal funds without a total dollar reduction in treatment.

States report very little reallocation of funds among functions within the mental health part of the block grant. All funding by law must go to CMHCs, and the funds continue to support the entire array of CMHC operations that prevailed before the block grant. Federally supported CMHCs faced annual cuts under the main grant program as part of the phasing out of this support after eight (or thirteen) years. Thus states had no need to reallocate among centers in order to cut funds still lower; they could live with the block-grant cuts simply by not going beyond eight years for current recipients and by making only limited, if any, new commitments. Some states did make CMHCs change their previous pattern of operations somewhat, however.

Consolidation of Program Administration

Administrative consolidation was natural under the ADM block grant for two reasons. First, states had even more involvement with ADM programs before the block grant than they had for the MCH or PHHS block grants. With only one exception, each of the sample states operated its own programs (with its own funds) in alcoholism, in drug abuse, and in community mental health before receiving the block grant. Second, direct federal grants (in alcoholism and community mental health) had been more common than in MCH or PHHS categorical programs and also more nearly duplicated state efforts, in effect supporting parallel programs that might naturally be folded into existing state systems. This provided an opportunity for relatively easy consolidation not available in the MCH or PHHS block grants.

It is therefore not surprising that all eighteen states consolidated the federal ADM programs into their existing state systems. Consolidation brought all federal dollars within a state-local framework, since local governments (usually counties) often help plan and finance services, which are typically delivered at the local level. State officials found this a natural move: they obviously liked their own systems, and staff could easily accommodate more funds and more service-provider grantees within a familiar process. They also thought it only fair that formerly direct federal grantees be treated the same as state grantees. In some cases, the officials also disliked the direct federal recipients' independence and were eager to have them observe state priorities.

The consolidation of a formerly dual system has had two main effects. First, it has achieved minor administrative efficiencies at all levels. Duplication of effort has been reduced by vastly lowering federal involvement while only moderately adding to the states' burden. States report that the marginal cost of having to administer more funds to more grantees was outweighed by eliminating provider and funding duplication. States could not document any sizable savings in this or other respects, but all felt that paperwork had been reduced and the funding process streamlined. It is interesting to note that state officials did not always like this savings: while they typically praised the lesser federal data reporting requirements, at the same time they usually complained that a national data base should have been retained—not to hold them to national standards but to allow them to make their own comparisons with other states' efforts. Some federal data collection would clearly be welcome, although individual states would surely have different visions of an ideal system.

Administrative savings from consolidation may have been greatest at the local level, according to state-level interviewees in the sample states. Local service-provider grantees receiving both state and federal funds in the past (including grantees in all three ADM program areas) can now receive these funds with a single application, under a single set of eligibility standards, and with only one set of reporting requirements (typically less detailed than previous federal ones). Further, in the numerous states in which alcoholism and drug abuse programs are administered within a single agency, applicants for both types of funds can usually submit a single "substance abuse" application instead of separate alcoholism and drug abuse service requests. Here, too, precise estimates of savings are impossible, but some most definitely occurred.

Former direct federal service-provider grantees that did not also receive state support did not save in the consolidation of two reporting processes into one; to the contrary, the need to deal with a different and unfamiliar process probably increased their administrative costs, at least in the initial transition year. However, states' officials at least claim that local service-provider grantees had no difficulties during the transition and that state requirements often seem somewhat less costly to meet in the long run. Local providers themselves are less optimistic about administrative savings. Our survey of local providers in three states included twelve ADM organizations. Spokespersons for two organizations said state requirements were less costly than federal; five organizations reported more costs; and five indicated no change or "unclear."

The second effect of consolidation has been either to make former service-provider grantees of federal funds better serve state priorities or to redirect funds away from them. At least nine of the eighteen sample states had made substantial shifts of this sort by the block grant's second year (as opposed, for example, to simply passing through a pro-rata share of block-grant funds to former grantees, a common first-year strategy). Such shifts nearly always placed the former grantees at a disadvantage, especially those that had not also previously received state support. All CMHCs, many alcoholism service-providers, and a few drug abuse agencies fall into this category as former direct recipients of federal funds. However, the federal rules protect many CMHCs, and states generally maintained almost all of former grantees' funding. Direct alcoholism and drug abuse service-provider grantees were unprotected by federal regulation and hence much more vulnerable to loss of block-grant funds or state aid and more likely to experience major shifts in service policy. More of them faced changes than did CMHCs, especially alcoholism service providers.

Most states are implementing new policies gradually, giving federal grantees an opportunity to adapt. In these states, funding levels of grantees are being "stepped down" over a period of several years, and shifts from advance grants to reimbursements are being implemented incrementally. Even where states have given counties control over provider selection, staff claim the federally funded providers are not receiving abrupt funding cuts by counties; apparently many CMHCs had provided state and locally funded services before the block grant and thus were familiar with the county systems. Indeed, in the sample states only isolated cases were observed in which grantees lost federal funding completely or even experienced abrupt major reductions (Texas' approach provides an example of the latter). However, as state consolidation plans become fully implemented, direct grantees will come under increased pressure to adapt or risk losing support.

Appendix A

Data on PHHS Initiatives

TABLE 35

STATE REDISTRIBUTIVE INITIATIVES UNDER THE PREVENTIVE HEALTH AND
HEALTH SERVICES BLOCK GRANT, SELECTED STATES, STATE FISCAL
YEARS 1982 AND 1983

Type of Incentives and State	Description
Mini-blocks	
Oregon	Consolidated all block-grant funds, except those reserved for Hypertension, Rape Prevention and Emergency Medical Services (EMS). Consolidated funds were distributed per capita to all counties.
Illinois[a]	Separate funding for the Rodent Control, Fluoridation, Home Health, and Health Education and Risk Reduction (HE/RR) programs was eliminated. Consolidated all PHHS funds except Hypertension and Rape Prevention. Funds distributed per capita to regions to be passed through to counties.
Ohio	Combined the 314(d), HE/RR and Rodent Control program funds into a mini-block but continued Fluoridation, EMS, Hypertension, and Rape Prevention on a categorical basis. Funds were distributed to counties statewide on a per capita basis.
North Carolina[b]	State fiscal 1984 plans include a mini-block of 314(d), Hypertension, and HE/RR program funds. Fluoridation, EMS, and Rape Prevention programs will be funded as separate categories. Under this plan the distribution of funds will not change, but instead counties will receive

131

TABLE 35 (*Continued*)

Type of Incentives and State	Description
	funding in proportion to their previous grant support from these three programs. Counties will have discretion over use of the funds (with the possible exception of Hypertension program dollars, due to the federal mandate) and over service providers. Although it will remain outside the mini-block, EMS grant distribution will change. Still restricted to EMS programs, these funds will be awarded by formula, instead of on a project basis, to regional agencies for distribution to local service-provider grantees.
Texas	Combined funds from equipment allocations of 314(d), Rodent Control, and EMS programs to create a local mini-block in state fiscal 1983. Funds are distributed statewide to counties according to the old 314(d) formula.
Other redistributions Massachusetts	Awards PHHS funds categorically, decreasing the award amounts to raise the number of grants. State administrators say this change allows them to expand these programs beyond just a few urban centers and create a broader availability of services.
Missouri	Shifted its formerly localized Hypertension program to a statewide network wherein every county receives some of these funds. Like Massachusetts, Missouri hoped to improve the program by broadening its coverage. However, state administrators believe that Hypertension program resources have been spread too thin, and that Missouri offers services where the need is low at the expense of targeting the higher-need urban areas. This program will return to its preblock competitive distribution practice in state fiscal 1984.

SOURCE: Based on telephone interviews with state health officials conducted in 1983.

a. Illinois received no EMS program funds in federal fiscal 1981, the base year, and thus had none allocated for EMS from the block grant.

b. North Carolina does not have Rodent Control or Home Health programs.

Appendix B

Data on ADM Block-Grant Requirements

TABLE 36

Major Requirements of the Alcohol, Drug Abuse, and Mental Health Block Grant

Category	Requirement
Overall	Each state must divide its ADM funds between substance abuse (alcohol and drugs) and mental health areas in proportion to each area's historical share of funds received. For mental health, historical share is based on federal fiscal 1981; for substance abuse, federal fiscal 1980 (before recisions). All 1982 funds were to be divided this way; in federal fiscal 1983 it was only 95 percent.
	No more than 10 percent of ADM funds may be spent for administrative purposes.
Community mental health	States must fund all CMHCs that received operational funds in federal fiscal 1981; these CMHCs would have remained eligible in 1982 had the categorical program continued (1981 was not the last year of their federal funding cycle). These protected centers need not receive the same *level* of funds, however. All other CMHCs may receive funding at state option.
	Block grant funds could not be spent on inpatient care.

TABLE 36 (*Continued*)

Category	Requirement
Substance abuse[a]	At least 70 percent of substance abuse funds (see above) must be divided equally between alcohol and drug functions. Each is thus assured 25 percent of the substance abuse funds, leaving only 30 percent for states to allocate at their discretion. At least 20 percent of ADM substance abuse funds must be spent on prevention or early intervention programs.

SOURCE: Based on Omnibus Budget Reconciliation Act of 1981.

a. Following congressional usage, wherein the term *substance abuse* includes both alcohol and drug abuse functions.